THE ULT KIDS GUIDE TO — LIFE SKILLS

101+ Practical Tools for Unlocking Potential and Broadening Children's Horizons for a Brighter Future

Grace Ann Grow

For every child stepping into the new era,
may this book be your compass
in a world of endless possibilities.
Let curiosity and kindness guide you
towards bright horizons!

Table of Contents

Appeal to Parents, Guardians, and Educators

Are you a parent, guardian, or educator? If so, you have an important role in shaping your child's personality—teaching them life skills for a thrilling and successful future. Now that it's your turn to teach these vital skills, *The Ultimate Kids' Guide to Life Skills* is the perfect tool for you!

The world around us is changing rapidly, and today's life demands more than academic knowledge. We often think about how to prepare our kids for life's challenges—all the things that schools don't teach. We all strive to raise confident, adaptive, and flourishing children under any circumstances. *The Ultimate Kids' Guide to Life Skills* is your trusted companion in this complex task.

Targeting children aged 8–12, this book teaches a wide array of essential life skills, helping young children learn about personal growth, emotional intelligence, and practical competence in daily life. This will help your child become adaptive, confident, and successful in facing the challenges of the modern world. Your child will come out feeling empowered with both practical knowledge and tools for navigating all aspects of life. This book instills confidence in your children to build their capacity for self-discovery and develop their strengths and talents uniquely.

I am Grace Ann Grow, a seasoned educator with more than two decades of experience in the educational field. I have long since been involved in the continuous development of educational programs for the holistic development of students. I strongly believe in inspiring children and caregivers to master essential life skills. My commitment to developing social skills, emotional intelligence, and self-discipline in elementary and middle school is the cornerstone of my remarkable work and achievement.

Coming from a family of teachers, my passion for teaching and belief in the potential of every child is deeply rooted in my upbringing. I have participated in educational initiatives, conducted workshops and seminars for educators and parents, and shared my ideas and experience with parents—and I am willing to share that with you and your children as well! My goal is to contribute to raising a generation of independent, confident, and happy children.

The content in this guide is valuable and in-depth, straight to the point, and presented logically, connecting one skill to another. Its writing style makes reading enjoyable for your kids. This book isn't just theoretical; it's filled with practical tips, too. Big terminologies that might seem overwhelming for your kids are broken down into basic and fun concepts.

There are no dry or academic presentations; it features practical activities, reflection questions, interactive exercises, games, and performance tasks. Each chapter has one or more of these features, and paragraphs are kept short and simple.

Now is a good time to teach your kids important life skills! You want your children to be respected by others and treated as equally important. Don't miss the opportunity to give your child the advantage they deserve in this rapidly changing world.

Start this trip today to secure your child's bright and successful future. Yes, this is the best guide for your children, vital for their personal fulfillment and real-world success!

Introduction

Hey buddy! Do you love adventures?

Then, get ready for a breathtaking cruise and an interactive adventure! You won't be journeying into the Kalahari Desert, nor will the trip take you to beautiful Disneyland. So, where is the destination heading? Here is a preview: It's a unique trip you will enjoy—a fascinating treasure trove of knowledge about life!

Oh! Life? Yes. Living life is one big adventure! But wait a moment, what do you think about life? Don't go too far. Just imagine you've somehow ended up in a dense forest with giant trees. You are filled with the fear of getting lost. No flashlights, no starlight, just thick darkness. Sure, it can feel creepy! What will you do? Will you choose a random path that might end up just anywhere?

What if you find a trusted adult who walks up with a map and shows you how to navigate your way? What if the adult didn't just promise to help you find the right path with the map but also pledged to walk with you and make the journey fun with great stories? Would you want to go with them?

Okay, come back home. What is the point of this imagination? This is it: Life is just like finding yourself in a dense forest, and you may need a guide; someone with the map to lead you to the right path. Life moves pretty fast! You've quickly grown from a helpless, cute newborn to a toddler and now to an adolescent heading off into the world.

As a tween, you have no prior experience with adulthood, yet you want to do what's right, and I respect your choice. I know you want to handle life more independently, and there is no better time to prepare for that than now! This is the time to get set for modern life. But how would you be able to do that?

That's the goal of this book! I want to be your friendly mentor and offer this book as your ultimate guide to life skills.

Let's get a good start here: What exactly are life skills?

Life skills are basic skills needed for taking care of yourself, getting through each day, and being efficient. These skills are needed for a better lifestyle for yourself and your loved ones. You can also view life skills as the abilities that assist you in living and succeeding in your daily life. Not having these skills can make it hard to do things on your own and handle basic tasks.

You are at the best stage in your life to learn these different skills. Do you know why? Because you have plenty of time to practice them before adulthood comes knocking on your door. You probably have a question running through your mind now: Why are life skills critical?

Imagine you can quote Shakespeare at the speed of light but can't sew a button. Quoting Shakespeare is impressive, but that wouldn't fix your lovely shirt. Will it? No! So, there is no doubt that life skills help us keep life running smoothly.

Buddy, your life is far too precious to live casually.

The *Ultimate Kids' Guide to Life* has 18 sections to help you understand crucial life skills. You will have a good start on mastering self-awareness, emotional magic, the art of social skills, valuing diversity, problem-solving skills, strategies to overcome bullies, the secrets of self-discipline, how to handle home responsibilities, and healthy lifestyles that you can adopt.

Moving ahead, this guide will teach you the basics of emergency and safety, how to navigate through the world of technology, and how to develop essential study habits and research skills. You will also learn the secrets of successful learning, the basics of financial literacy, how to effectively navigate the world of hobbies and games, the basics of surviving and exploring nature, mastering environmental responsibility, contributing to society and the world at large, and securing your journey to continuous self-improvement.

Did I just hear you say, "Hey, it's a complete package!"? You're right! This book is written for you: No complex grammar; just simple phrases, fun stories, and real-life experiences that bring the points to life. Then, you will find hints and actionable tips for effective implementation. Trust me, you won't navigate this journey alone.

This book will help you fully understand the critical skills that are foundational for your personal goals. It will help you build strong relationships and effectively develop problem-solving skills, setting the stage for a satisfying and successful life!

Learning these skills will give you an edge in the future, helping you adapt and thrive. You need this to shape your path, navigate challenges, and seize pleasant opportunities. Kudos to your parents or caregivers for investing in this book for you. There's no doubt they love you very much.

Finally, I want to tell you that taking you through this exciting journey brings me extreme pleasure. I am confident you will apply all the lessons, arming yourself with the crucial skills to survive adulthood in style!

Chapter 1: Your Inner Compass—Discovering Self-Awareness

From the moment you were born, your journey of knowing yourself started. You started to touch, listen, and speak. While your journey of self-awareness begins from birth, you need to regularly learn about yourself to discover who you really are and what makes you unique. But how will you find this out in.

You will find out with the help of your inner compass. Just like how sailors use the compass to find their way on the ocean, your inner compass will help you understand who you are. This chapter aims to help you find and follow your inner compass. So, let's set sail for this exciting journey!

Getting to Know Yourself: Who Are You and Why Are You the Way You Are?

Knowing yourself—which is called self-awareness—is a journey, and you will continue to do that for the rest of your life. So, what exactly is self-awareness? It is the ability to know, understand, and tag your thoughts, emotions, and behaviors. It helps you to be in tune with your abilities, your mistakes, what you cherish, and what you trust.

A person who is not self-aware is like someone in a deep sleep. A person in a deep sleep is not aware of what is close to them. That means, to be self-aware, you need to know yourself.

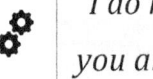

> **Consider this:**
> *When someone asks, "Why did you do that?" if you say, "I do not know," what does that mean? It means that you are not self-aware. But if you ask the same question to a more self-aware person, how will they answer? They will likely say, "I did this because..."*

How to Become Self-Aware

Create Time and Space for Self-Reflection

You can do this by walking outside, sitting down, or just lying down, thinking about your actions and characters.

> **Hint:**
> *While it might seem like you are doing nothing, you are actually processing information and learning about yourself.*

Get a Journal

Write down your thoughts in a journal to safely express how you feel. It should include how you feel, what you think, and what frightens or inspires you.

> **Hint:**
> *You can combine words with either images or drawings for clarity.*

What Self-Awareness Looks Like

Joey was having difficulty doing his assignment. He needed help from his mom. However, his mom was busy getting dinner ready in the kitchen.

Joey didn't ask for help because he did not want to interrupt his mom. He knew that getting frustrated would not help him do his assignments better. He remembered that he could do other assignments that were not taxing. Then, after dinner, Mom could help him with the assignment.

Without self-awareness, Joey would have interrupted his mom, and if his mother suggested that he go for another, less difficult, assignment, Joey could become frustrated.

Your Talents: How to Find and Grow Them

You have a friend who has been with you since birth. Do you want to know that friend? Well, the friend is your talent. Everyone is born with talents, and we need to grow and develop this talent. The tricky thing, though, is that we are not good at finding this friend. But don't worry—there is a way around it.

Our talents might range from sense, arts, and communication with others, to athletic abilities. Mind you, your talent does not have to bring you money, popularity, fun, or more.

How Do You Find Your Talents?

What You Enjoy Most

What you enjoy doing, are attracted to, or like practicing can be your natural talent. So, let me ask: Do you enjoy dancing, painting, singing, engaging in sports, or playing a musical instrument? These or other activities you love can be your natural talents.

> **Hint:**
> *Find out what activities you enjoyed most in the past few months.*

What You Do Easily

Is there anything you find really easy to do, like a cakewalk, while others find it hard? These can be your natural talents! For example, do you find it easy to solve puzzles, while other kids find it hard? That could be your talent and a pointer to a career choice.

Ask People

Your mom, dad, and older siblings can be your source for an honest assessment about what they think your talent is. Ask lots of people and note their comments. Then, compile the results and compare them with what you already thought. Trust me, it might be your hidden talent.

What to Keep in Mind When Finding Your Talents

- **Do not rush the process:** Take the search easy. For instance, it can take you days to discover your talents. Do not be satisfied with just a few talents in your journal. You have many talents. So, take your time.

- **Focus on only the best:** You will eventually come up with a long list. The next step is to pick the ones that appeal to you the most. Focus on talents that you are excited to learn about.

Your Weaknesses: How to Understand and Improve Them

Caleb is overly emotional and moody and cries over the least problem. One day, when an ambulance speeds by, Caleb starts crying. He knows that someone is hurt inside.

Is being overly emotional and moody a weakness? Maybe so! But if we look deeper, could that weakness be turned into a strength? Absolutely.

How can Caleb be helped? First, Caleb has to know that crying over the least problem is a weakness. That step is important in identifying one's strengths and improving oneself

So yes, we have figured out Caleb's weakness, but could this weakness tell us something about Caleb? Yeah! It could mean Caleb is genuinely aware of his weakness and cares for others. These are Caleb's strengths! And yeah, he can use this strength to become a better human.

Like Caleb, you have weaknesses too. You can find them by paying more attention to yourself. What are some of the weaknesses a child can have? Here are some:

- talkativeness

- clinginess

- noncooperation

- fear

- silliness

- loudness

- pride

- back talk

- quietness

- shyness

- bossiness

If you have any of these traits, they are your weaknesses. But can they be turned to strengths? Yes! Examine the chart below for a start:

Weakness	Strength
Clingy	Affectionate
Talkative	Good communicator
Fearful	Careful or thoughtful
Defiant	Courageous, strong beliefs
Silly	Entertaining
Loud	Confident
Shy	Deep thinker
Bossy	Serious
Quiet	Thinker
Back talk	Courageous

How to Transform Your Weaknesses to Strengths

To transform your weaknesses into areas to improve and areas of strength, take these steps:

- **Admit that you are not perfect:** Your first step to transforming weaknesses into strengths is knowing you are imperfect. This thought can make you pause and check yourself.

- **Make an honest list of weaknesses:** The next step is to list and label your weaknesses. Once you have admitted them, you will become fairer.

- **Find where a weakness can give rise to real value:** Once you identify your weakness, you can think better. Then, you can think of the positive side of those negative traits and where they can help.

Things Important to You: What You Value and Believe In

What moves Mom and Dad to make decisions every morning? Why does your teacher act the way they do? What drives people's actions? The simple answer: Beliefs and values!

Values (or what you find precious) are like a tour guide who leads you to the right place. They help you determine right from wrong, what is important, and how you should live. These values can come from your culture, beliefs, and experiences.

Some common values include respect, honesty, loyalty, and compassion. If you break a flower vase and Mom asks, "What happened?" what decision would you make? If you hold on to the value of honesty, you will be more inclined to speak the truth even if Mom gets angry at you. If you say the truth over and over, honesty or being truthful will become your identity. People can now say, "Oh! He's truthful in whatever he says."

But the big question is: How can you identify your values and beliefs?

How to Find Your Values and Beliefs

- **Your interactions with others:** In school, at home, and when with friends, what you do will reflect your values. When a friend is hurt, how do you respond? What if you offend your sibling? Will you be willing to say sorry? Pay attention to your interactions with others. They can be a great signal.

- **What others say about you:** What do you often hear from siblings, classmates, parents, and others? Is there a behavior they usually say you have? For example, do your parents and teachers always talk about your kindness or honesty? Any of the attitudes they mention regularly point to the value you love.

- **Use value sorting cards:** Make cards with written values like kindness, courage, integrity, and honesty. Ask your parents to sort the cards that best describe your identity.

How to Build Great Values

- **Read novels:** There are novels with moral situations. As you read, pause and ask questions. You can say, "If I was in this person's position, what would I have done?"

- **Use digital apps:** Ask Mom and Dad to recommend apps that teach values. They come with scenarios that require responses from users.

Thinking About Yourself: Why You Act the Way You Do

Dan suddenly starts to sob. Other pupils and teachers do not know why Dan is so upset that he cannot talk. After some time, the teacher realizes that Dan has challenges with the assignment.

Let me ask you: If Dan had a better self-introspection, would he have taken a break, tried a better approach, or asked for help when the frustration was rising? I suppose you'll say yes! Let's now explore practical ways to engage in self-understanding.

The Importance of Self-Introspection

Self-introspection—that is, thinking back on past events—is a skill you should learn. Below are some points on the importance of learning self-introspection:

- **Great understanding:** It can help you understand your feelings and thoughts, know who you are, and improve your happiness.

- **An invaluable skill for knowing yourself:** It is the only skill that can help you understand why you think or feel like you do.

- **Enhances empathy:** You can strengthen empathy (feeling for others) with introspection. If you can empathize with your friend because they broke their toy, you can better understand yourself. This is because you are putting yourself in their shoes.

Practical Ways to Think Back on Past Events

Here are practical ways you can think back about the events in your past:

- **Ask "what" questions:** You are not too young to ask yourself "what" questions. In fact, starting now can help you a lot in the future. "What" questions are more effective in enhancing your introspection. For example, when you are sad, instead of saying, "Why am I sad?" ask, "What is making me sad?" Using "what" will help you understand your feelings better.

- **Extend your views:** You have to be curious about your inner self. This curiosity can help you better understand how you feel. If you are curious about what makes you angry, you can better avoid anger. When someone is about to upset you, you can find a way to avoid that situation.

- **Let your mind be quiet:** You need to calm your mind to understand how it works. The more quiet time you have, the better you will understand yourself.

Being Unique: How to Be Yourself

Television, the kids in school, and other factors can affect how you view beauty, career choices, and success. But now is the time to accept how special you are. After all, it is no longer news that you are unique.

What will help you be yourself? Self-love! Self-love can help you build a positive sense of who you are. It will help you steer clear of comparing yourself to others.

How You Can Develop a Good Sense of Uniqueness

So, let's run through tips on how you can develop that.

Fight Negative Language and Thoughts

Some thoughts and words make you lose what you care about and trust. So, do not get involved in harmful thoughts or language.

- **Example 1:** Suppose you are working on a craft at home with your sibling. Even if your painting does not come out the way you like, do not say, "This doesn't look cool." Instead, engage in words like, "My sibling and I displayed our creativity in different ways. It's good to come up with a new approach."

- **Example 2:** Suppose you're playing football with some kids at school and you didn't score a goal. If negative thoughts like "I didn't play well today" pop into your head, change them to positive statements like "I dribbled past many players today. I did well."

Self-Reflection Can Help

If you compare yourself to others, it will steal your joy. So, do not go down that lane. Every day, reflect on what you love about yourself. Once you figure that out, draw a picture of it.

> **Here is an idea:**
> *Do you like the birthmark on your shoulder? Can you draw it? It could also be something you think about often. If drawing isn't your thing, just write it down.*

Be Clear

When praising yourself, be specific. Rather than saying, "I did a good job," "I am great," or, "That is amazing," try saying something like, "What a great job I did with memorizing my lines," or "I did well explaining the story at school today." By being specific, you will identify your special skills and strengths.

What an insight into the inner compass! Remember, getting to know yourself, finding your talents, understanding your weaknesses, self-reflection, and staying unique will keep your inner compass active!

Interestingly, emotional intelligence (being smart with your feelings) is one of the aspects of self-awareness. So, what exactly is it? Let's explore that in the next chapter!

Chapter 2: Emotion Magic— Emotional Intelligence Journey

An emotion is how you feel inside of you. What about emotional intelligence, then? I'll help: It is your ability to notice, manage, and understand how you and others feel.

>
> **Consider this:**
> *David's friend got bad news. He asked David if they could stop playing. David gets it and goes home.*

Is this a big deal? Yes! It means David is super smart with his feelings.

You can be like David! In this chapter, you will improve your emotional intelligence. You will learn how to manage and understand your feelings. You will also learn to talk out, recognize, and direct your feelings. These include sadness, joy, fear, and anger.

> **Here's a tip:**
> *Getting started with a bowl of popcorn is a good idea!*

Understanding Your Feelings: What Are Feelings, and Why Do They Matter?

We must know our feelings. We must accept them. We must also accept those of others. Emotional awareness involves the following:

- **Awareness:** Imagine you're in a forest, and you see a new animal. This animal is like a feeling that has just arrived. You notice it and tell yourself, "Hey, there's something new here!"

- **Labeling:** Now, you give that animal a name. You look closely and say, "This one is called 'Happy,' and that one is 'Sad.'"

- **Finding out:** You start to search where this animal came from. Did it come from a fun game you are playing, or maybe because your toy is missing? You search to know why the feeling appeared.

- **Express:** You show the new animal to your friends. You might say, "Look, I'm feeling Happy because I found my toy!" or "I'm feeling Sad because I cannot find my toy."

- **Regulation control:** An animal might be too big and roaring. So, if the feeling is too big, like a big Angry tiger, you need to calm it down. Take deep breaths or talk to someone to help you feel better.

How Emotional Awareness Works

Let's combine these five steps to learn how emotional awareness works.

Imagine that something happens to Kate. Maybe Kate sees a big, scary dog. Kate's eyes and ears send a message to a part of her brain. It works like an alarm, and this makes Kate feel scared.

Kate's initial reaction: Kate might feel her heart racing or might want to run away.

Now, a part of Kate's brain will help her think about what's happening. It will make her understand, "Oh, I'm scared."

So here, Kate will name the feeling. She will tell herself, "I'm scared because of the dog."

Finally, she will manage her reactions. Now that Kate knows she's scared, she can calm down by taking deep breaths or asking an adult for help.

Using Kate's illustration, you will notice that being aware of emotions has three parts. First is the initial response. Then comes identifying the emotion. Last is managing it.

I will not teach you how to express all your feelings. But I will mention some ways to express your feelings. These examples will teach you how to manage others.

Knowing and Expressing Your Feelings

- **Happiness:** You feel happy when something good happens to you. For example, you will be happy if you get a good grade. When you are happy, you will

  - smile
  - laugh
  - feel calm
  - play well with friends

- **Anger:** You feel anger when someone does not treat you well. For example, if your friend hits you, you might be angry. When you are angry, you will

  - cry

  - yell

  - hit

  - throw a toy across the room

These are just two of the feelings you will feel. There are more. So, to know and express them, ask yourself each time you experience something:

- What is happening in my body?

- How am I feeling?

- What thought am I having?

Provide answers to these questions. You can ask Mom, Dad, or an older adult to show you an emotion card or chart. It will help you name these feelings.

When You Get Angry: How to Calm Down and Express It Right

Anger is a feeling. This emotion has a purpose. Showing it well can offer many health benefits. In this section, you will dig deeper into anger and learn what you can do when you feel angry.

Let's start with this question: *What exactly can make you angry?*

Many things can make you angry, but here are the basics:

- hunger
- loud noises
- when you have to share toys with other people
- when you cannot tell how you feel, or need help understanding what is happening or knowing the right words
- when you can't control how you feel
- when you can't get what you want
- when you feel that something is not fair
- when your parents discipline you
- when you cannot get what you want
- when your mom, dad, siblings, friends, or teachers misunderstand you, handing you unjust treatment
- when people reject you

How Kids Display Anger

You can display anger by

- throwing tantrums

- crying

- bullying or hurting others

- using abusive language to cause harm

- kicking

- hitting

- having a red face

How to Calm Down When Angry

It is okay to be angry, worried, or sad. But hurting others or yourself is not okay. Before you start getting angry, it's good to know some signs that can tell you that anger is setting in. When anger starts to build up, you might notice that

- your heart is beating faster

- your muscles become tense

- your stomach makes a sound

- you start to grit your teeth

Once you notice any of these signs, the next step is to manage it. You can do that by

- walking away from what is making you angry

- counting from 1 to 10

- breathing slowly and deeply

- talking to a trusted person, like your mom, dad, or older siblings

- finding a spot in a home where you can go to calm down

- drawing something funny

- writing on a piece of paper and tearing it up

- bringing the palms of your hands together, pushing, and releasing

- performing stretches

These tips can help you handle anger the right way.

Feeling Sad or Let Down: Ways to Feel Better

This is what sadness looks like in a child:

- **Old fun isn't fun anymore:** What you used to love, like playing games, might be less fun.

- **School doesn't matter as much:** You might care about school less than before.

- **Feel sick:** You could get more tummy aches and headaches.

- **Tears come easily:** You might cry more often, even over small things.

- **Lots of complaints:** You might have lots of complaints.

Now that you know what sadness feels like, let's get to the fun part: How can you overcome sadness?

How to Overcome Sadness

You can cope with sadness with these strategies:

- **Name your feelings:** An emotion card is a simple visual representation that showcases various feelings and emotions. These cards can include words and images that help clarify how we feel at any moment. Use the emotion card to find your feelings. Once that is done, name it. For example, it can be as simple as saying, "Right now, I am feeling sad." If you know why, say, "I am sad because I did not do well on my test."

- **Know that you are not alone:** When you are sad, think about others in the same situation. Using the earlier example, you can say, "I am not the only child who did not do well." This can help you stay calm.

- **Take calm belly breaths:** Close your eyes and allow your belly to expand by breathing in. Then, breathe all the air out. After doing that three to four times, notice how you feel. It will reduce your sadness.

- **Be positive:** Don't give up when things do not go your way. For example, "I am sad now because I did not do well, but there are other tests where I performed well," or "Does this failure show where I can do better?" Questions like these will help you stay positive. They will also help you learn about the situation.

When Should You Seek Help

If you have tried these steps and still feel upset, then get support.

Tell someone how you feel: For example, tell your family or friends. They will listen to you. Once you are done talking, they will say, "Now I see why you feel that way." Most of the time, that may be all you need. Sometimes, you may need to talk more.

You must spend time with the person until you feel better. They might even ask you to do something fun to relieve you of your sadness.

Being Scared or Worried: How to Feel Braver

Ed was scared of thunderstorms and lightning when he was eight years old. He said, "During a thunderstorm, I'll always run to my parents' bed. But now that I am older, I run outside each time there is a storm."

Like Ed, you will have something you fear. So, do this: Write down some of the things you fear.

Are you done? Okay. Now, compare your list with this:

- a dark room
- a neighbor's dog
- heights
- strangers
- getting hurt
- getting sick

- bullies

- sports

Did you find something similar on your list? That's okay! This goes to show that you are not alone.

How to Overcome Anxiety and Fears

- **Take time out:** When you are anxious or feeling scared, take time out to calm down. Stay away from what you are afraid of. For example:

  - Drink a glass cup of water.

  - Go have a bath.

  - Do a breathing exercise.

- **Breathe through the fear:** If you're sweating or your heart is racing, put your palms on your stomach. Then, breathe in deeply and slowly.

- **Face it:** If you avoid your fear, it will make it worse. For example, if you fear getting into an elevator, go do it the very next day. Whatever the fear is, face it.

- **Fight unhelpful thoughts:** Ask the right questions. For instance, if you fear swimming, ask yourself:

  - Have I heard of a child drowning while swimming? Was someone there to watch the child, and was the child wearing swimming gear?

- Is there a reason to feel like I will drown?

- **Visualize happy places:** Close your eyes and imagine a safe place. You can imagine

  - a peaceful beach

  - a good memory from childhood

  - moments with your pets

- **Talk about it:** Share how you feel with someone who can make it funny or push you to face it.

- **Reward yourself:** You achieved something you once feared! Now, you can

  - treat yourself to a meal

  - play a game

  - ask your parents to reward you for facing your fears

Keeping Calm: Tips for Less Stress

Stress is when you feel worried about something. For example, having too much homework or a fight with a friend. It can hurt your tummy, make you feel tired, or make you want to cry.

The first step is to reduce the things that make you stressed. After that, you can develop the power to face the stress you cannot avoid.

Methods for Reducing Stress

- **Find out the reason for your stress:** When you feel pressured, take a moment to find the cause of your feelings. The more you know the cause, the easier you can avoid it. If school assignments stress you out, talk to your parents. They will be ready to help.

- **Use art therapy:** Sometimes, you *must* face stress. So, use art therapy. Okay, this is not just about coloring. It involves creative works. These include writing stories. They also include drawing, singing, and dancing.

- **Play:** You can minimize stress by playing more often. Spend time with nature. For example, can you watch nature documentaries? These can be about some rare animals.

- **Use the Calm app:** Ask Mom and Dad to get some nice apps to calm you.

How to Build Emotional Resilience—The Ability to Cope with Bad Situations

Imagine that Mom drops an egg or spills some milk on the floor. Then she says, "Oh, no, this is a mess, and I am in a hurry." The next moment, she cleans the mess with no further complaints.

Or consider this scenario. Mom's blouse got ripped. She wanted to wear it with her slacks. What will she do? She goes, "Oh! What will I do now! Is it time to leave? Okay, I will figure something out now." And boom, she did!

You will notice that Mom coped well with the stress in both scenarios. Here is the lesson:

Your parents are a great resource. They provide emotional strength. Watch them more.

Other Ways to Cope with Unpleasant Situations

- **Engage and connect with others:** You will listen more and get help as you talk.

- **Take a break:** Get creative with something else.

- **Practice self-care:** Engage in regular exercise. Eat a balanced diet and get enough rest.

- **Set goals:** It can be as simple as saying "please and thank you" daily. You can also break big assignments into small tasks.

Thinking Happy Thoughts: How to Stay Positive

Life is not fair. You must make it fair. You can do this with positive thinking, even in hard times.

Turning Unpleasant Situations into Good Ones

- **See the good side of hard situations:** There is no excuse for bullies. But are there any lessons to learn? Hear this from Ben: *"Because I was bullied, I have been able to spot and deal with them. I can now stand up for myself and those around me."* So, for every difficult situation, see it as an opportunity to learn and grow.

- **Make daily gratitude a habit:** Think about what you can be grateful for daily. Think of anything Dad and Mom did for you or what you could do in school. This will help you pay attention to what you have.

- **Imagine a positive result:** If an assignment feels hard, imagine the result if you don't give up. Doing this will help you to keep going.

- **Break down tasks:** Sometimes, a task you find too big can become small if you break it into pieces. Did Mom ask you to help with the dishes? Can you start with all the cutlery, then move to the cups and the other plates? You will be happy to get the others done as you get one done.

What Can Help You Develop a Positive Attitude?

You can be more positive if you develop the following skills:

- **Practice Loving-Kindness Meditation:** Think about loved ones. This includes cousins. It also includes siblings. It includes aunts, uncles, and even friends. Then, write something nice and send it to them or give it to them when they come around.

- **Help others:** Do kind acts for others. It could be as simple as getting them a glass of water. You can pick up toys, help Mom in the kitchen, or do house chores without being told to do them.

- **Journaling:** Write down the amazing times you've had in your life.

- **Regularly say positive words:** This includes words like "I am a good friend," "I am kind," and "I am loving."

Managing Your Feelings: Ways to Keep Them in Check

You need self-regulation and self-control. They help you manage your feelings. Do these words seem like big terms? Let's break it down:

- **Self-control** is when you make yourself do the right thing, even if it's hard. For example, when you study for a test instead of watching your favorite show.

- **Self-regulation** is handling pressure. You control your strong wants for something. For example, you choose to read instead of watching a movie. Why? Because you know a bad grade will make Daddy say, "No TV during weekdays."

Now, let's talk about the methods for self-control.

Techniques for Self-Control

- **Practice good habits:** Sometimes, we don't want to do certain things. For instance, when your mom tells you that you can't have ice cream until after dinner and you don't cry or beg, that's called self-control. Each time you behave this way, you are showing self-control.

- **Take responsibility:** You lost a toy Mom has repeatedly asked you to put away. Don't cry for a new one.

- **Embrace limits:** It's okay to lose a benefit or get a timeout. This could be for disrespecting a sibling or speaking rudely. It will teach you to be careful with your actions or words.

- **Stop and think:** Before you make a choice, hit the pause button and think.

How to Practice Self-Regulation

These activities will enhance self-regulation in you:

- **Breathe intentionally:** Take deep breaths to focus and let the moment pass.

- **Adjust your sleep routine:** Sleep helps memory and behavior.

- **Play board games:** They teach the importance of taking turns, responding when you lose, and managing your feelings.

- **Rock (or roll):** When strong emotion sets in, you can rock back and forth. You can rock in a rocking chair or listen to soft music.

- **Use the 5–4–3–2–1 method:** After inhaling deeply, focus on your surroundings and observe what captures your attention. For example:

  A. Five things you can see

  B. Four things you can touch or feel

  C. Three things you can hear

  D. Two things you can smell

  E. One thing you can taste

These tips will make it easier to gain emotional intelligence. You can better manage your emotions.

In the next chapter, you will learn what you can do to develop social skills!

Chapter 3: Friendship Secrets—The Art of Social Skills

Do you want more playmates? Are you too shy to ask friends that you want to play? Do you sometimes feel lonely at school? If you said yes to any of these, I'm here to help!

Once, a boy named Joe felt the same way. He was shy and played alone until one day, he shared his colorful crayons with a new boy. They drew unicorns and rainbows together, and the boy said, "You're my best friend now!" Ever since that day, Joe has never been lonely.

Imagine the joy of making new friends like Joe did! It's a wonderful feeling that you can experience too!

Do you want to be like Joe? Welcome! Get ready for exciting stories, awesome tips, and laughter as we journey into the amazing world of friendship!

How People Connect: The Basics of Friendship and Cooperation

Okay, do you sometimes wonder why some kids have many friends? This is the secret: They know what is called "social dynamics." But don't worry, it's not as complicated as it sounds. Social dynamics is simply about how people talk, communicate, and become friends. It's something you can understand and master too!

Should we start with what Henry did?

Henry was just like you. He was too shy to talk to other kids. He did not know what to say and how to join others in playing games. But that's okay—we all feel shy sometimes. One day at recess, he saw Tim playing with a fine toy car. Henry wanted to play but did not know how to tell Tim.

But Henry remembered what Mom told him: "Start with a smile and a simple question." Then, Henry walked up to Tim, smiled, and asked, "Can I play with you?" Tim smiled back and gave Henry the toy car. They played, laughed, and, from then on, became best friends.

What did you learn? Start with a smile and ask a simple question.

What You Can Do to Connect with People

- When someone talks to you, listen to what they say.

- Don't wait for others to share with you; share your toys and games with others first. This will make them happy, and they'll want to be your friend.

- Even if you feel shy, be nice. Kindness can make others feel good and want to be around you.

- If you see kids playing a game, ask if you can join. Most kids will be happy to invite you.

Smile and Question Game

Next time you are at school or anywhere else:

- **Find someone:** Look for someone who isn't playing but wants to play.

- **Smile:** A big, friendly smile will show them you're nice and that you want to be their friend.

- **Ask a question:** It can be simple. For example: "Can I play with you?" or "What game are you playing?"

Try this a few times and see how it works. It might surprise you to find that you will make many new friends! Remember, it's as simple as smiling, asking a question, and having fun. That's all it takes to make a new friend!

Always pay attention to how other kids feel—their faces and looks. This will help you know when they are happy, sad, or want to play. Understanding how others feel is a superpower that will help you make friends and keep them.

Family Time: Why Getting Along at Home Matters

Learning to talk, listen, and share feelings with you is important because you love Dad, Mom, and your siblings. What you say and do while you are with them can help you when you go outside.

Let's see what happened to Lily and her family.

Lily loved her family, but sometimes, they did not understand her. This made Lily sad. One day, when feeling sad about a broken toy, she talked to her mom. Instead of crying, Lily calmly said, "Mom, I feel sad because I broke my toy. Can you help me?"

Her mom hugged her and said, "I'm sorry you're sad. Let's fix it together." Lily felt better. From that day, Lily learned that talking about her feelings is one of the best ways to deal with them.

Later, when her brother was angry about losing a game, Lily listened and said, "It's okay. Do you want to play a different game?" They played together and had fun.

How to Become More Friends with Everyone at Home

- **Speak up:** If you are worried, tell your family calmly.

- **Listen well:** When someone in your family is talking, listen carefully. It shows you care about their feelings.

- **Show respect:** Use kind words and be gentle, even when sad. It helps everyone stay calm.

- **Share feelings:** Don't be afraid to say how you feel. Whether you're happy, sad, or mad, sharing helps your family understand you better.

Family Chat Game

Show Mom and Dad this game and ask that all of you can play it together:

- **Pick a time:** Choose a time when everyone will be together, like during dinner or after school.

- **Take turns:** Each person shares something about their day. It can be anything—what made them happy, something they learned, or a problem they faced.

- **Listen:** While someone is talking, everyone else listens without responding. When they're done, you can ask questions or say something nice.

Always put yourself in your family members' shoes and imagine how they feel. Spend time playing games or having family meals. This will help you bond and understand each other better.

Talking and Listening: Sharing Thoughts and Feelings Effectively

To listen, you must hear what others are saying without saying a thing until they are done.

When talking, you have to speak gently, use good words, and notice the look of the person you are talking to.

These skills will help you make new friends and understand people better.

What Will Help You Communicate Well

- **Start a conversation:** Smile and say something like "hi!" You can also ask a simple question like, "How was your day?"

- **Listen well:** When your playmate or family talks, look at them and pay attention. Don't say anything until they ask you to.

- **Speak clearly:** Use nice words and speak clearly enough so others can hear you.

- **Watch for signs:** Look at their faces and what their behavior shows.

- **Share how you feel:** It's fine to say "I feel happy" or "I feel sad." This helps others understand you better.

Hands-On Activity: The Feelings Chart

- Ask Mom or Dad to make a feelings chart for you. You will use this to share how you feel every day.

- Put a sticker or draw a mark next to how you feel each day. Share your chart with your family and talk about how you feel about something.

- Using the feelings chart your parents gave you, add more feelings like surprise to the list.

- Let one person act out an emotion without saying a word. Then, allow others to guess. Compare the emotion with the chart.

The Listening Game

Duration for each topic: 60 seconds

Players:

- Minimum: 2

- Maximum: Unlimited

Instructions

- Pick something fun to talk about, like favorite games or animals.

- One person talks about the topic for one minute while the other listens.

- Now, the listener talks and the first person listens.

- After both have talked, share what you learned about each other.

Some questions that will let you talk and listen well:

- How do I feel when my playmate or family members listen to me?

- Do I benefit when I listen to others?

- Can I put my toys away to better listen to others?

All of these will help you to talk nicely and listen well.

Making Friends: How to Find and Keep Them

Now, let's talk more about how to make and keep new friends. First, how can you find friends? Let's check these four ways:

- **Join others:** During recess in school, join school clubs or sports. For example, you can join a soccer team or even an art club.

- **Compliment others:** Say nice things about someone's drawings or toys. For example, you can say, "Tony, your drawing is really cool!" or "I love your toy car!"

- **Share snacks:** Share your snacks during breaks with someone who does not have them. You can start by saying, "Would you like some of my cookies?"

- **Talk about what you love:** Show and talk about what you love. You might find someone who loves the same thing. For example, if you love cats, talk about them and find someone who loves cats too.

Behaviors for Good Friendship

- Be nice to each other.

- Tell the truth.

- Help each other when they are sad or need help.

- Enjoy spending time together and have fun.

Sometimes, your friends can do something you do not like. Therefore, talk out your feelings when you are angry. If you make mistakes, say "sorry." And finally, after you tell your friend sorry, do not repeat the mistakes.

Hands-On Activity

> **A simple task:**
>
> *Get a greeting card.*

Ask your parents for a greeting card. Write why a friend is special to you in the card and give it to them the next day at school. This activity shows your friends that you care about them.

Game: Friendship Bingo

Create a bingo card with different friendship activities like

- "Share a toy."
- "Say something nice."
- "Play a game together."
- "Listen to a friend."

Play the game with your friends, do each activity, and mark it.

The first one to get Bingo wins!

When Your Friend Travels

When your friend travels, it's okay to feel sad, but remember, you can always make new friends and keep in touch with old ones. To make new friends, remember to be friendly and kind.

Practice these skills and enjoy the fun of having great friends!

Understanding Others: Learning to Care and Share

To have more friends to play with, you need respect and empathy. Respect means doing to others what you want them to do to you. For example, would you want a friend to interrupt you if you are talking to them? No. It would help if you did the same when they spoke to show that you respect them.

Empathy means understanding how a person feels. For example, if your friend is sad, try to know why they are sad, and think about their situation as if you are the one it happened to. If your friend lost their toys, then imagine that you are the one who lost them.

Ways to Show Respect

- **Be a good listener:** When someone is talking to you, look at them. Wait to talk until they ask you.

- **Be nice:** Use words and actions like "please" and "thank you."

- **Follow the rules:** Respect the rules at home, at school, and when you're playing with friends.

How to Show Empathy

- **Pay attention to feelings:** Notice how your friends are feeling. Are they happy, sad, or angry?

- **Ask questions:** If you don't know how someone feels, ask them. For example, you can say, "Are you okay?" or "Do you want to talk?"

- **Help others:** If a friend is sad or needs help, offer to help them. Hug them when they are sad.

Story Time

Lily, who loves planting flowers, saw her friend looking sad. Instead of ignoring her, Lily asked, "Mary, are you okay?" Mary explained that she lost her favorite toy. Lily listened and offered to help her look for it. Together, they found the toy, and Mary felt much better.

Respect and empathy make your friends feel good and create strong, happy relationships!

Role-Playing Game

- Pair up with a friend or family member.

- Take turns acting out different scenarios where someone might need help. For example, one person might act like they have fallen and gotten hurt, another can act like they are left out, and another can act like they are feeling sad.

- Talk and practice what you can say and do to show you care in each situation.

Working Together: How to Be a Good Team Player

When you work together with others, you will be able to get things done faster and better. But that is not all: You will also be able to listen to how your friends get things done and how they play with their siblings.

These activities will help you develop problem-solving skills:

- **Play puzzles:** Work on jigsaw puzzles at home or with friends. As you play, listen to how your friends come up with and share ideas.

- **Create something:** Create something together, like a LEGO structure or a craft.

- **Play cooperative games:** Play games like "Escape Room" challenges or group board games.

- **Engage in role play:** Engage in role play where you need to solve a problem, like finding a lost item or planning a party.

- **Join sports teams:** Join a sports team where you can practice playing together and support teammates.

- **Engage in classroom activities:** When your teacher asks you to join others in a group activity, be ready to join.

- **Help with household chores:** Help anyone in the family with chores. For example, you can join others in setting the table or cleaning the dining.

By working with others, listening to them, and combining their strengths, you can solve problems more effectively.

Group Story Creation

- Sit in a circle with your team.

- One person starts a story with one sentence. Then, the next person adds another sentence.

- Keep going around the circle until the story is complete.

- Discuss how listening to each other's ideas made the story more interesting and creative.

Solving Problems Together with Others

- **Think together:** When there's a problem, sit down with friends or family and think of many solutions.

- **Ask questions:** Sometimes, if you do not know what to do, ask Mom and Dad.

- **Listen to others:** Pay attention to what your friends say and note their ideas and feelings.

- **Divide the task:** Sometimes, you need to break the problem into smaller parts and ask each person to solve different parts.

Solving Arguments: Finding Fair Solutions

Sometimes, you will not agree with your friends on toys, games, snacks, ideas, turns, seats, shows, and more.

But you want to keep your friend, right? Good! If you want to keep your friends, you must learn to resolve whatever makes you refuse to agree. There are things you can do.

The first thing you can do is to figure out why you do not agree with a friend. Is it because you want a different toy, because you do not understand what they say or do, or because they hurt you? What can you do if you're going to play a game and your sibling or friend wants to play the same game? Let me share Bright and Ben's story with you.

Bright and Ben wanted to use the same swing during recess. It was Bright that got there first. But Ben was angry because he wanted a turn, too. Ben shouted, "Bright, it's my turn!"

Bright replied, "I just got here. But how about we take turns? I will swing for 3 minutes; then you will swing for the same minutes. Caleb can watch the time for us."

Ben accepted. Caleb set the timer, and they each had their turns. What was the result?

They enjoyed the swing and had fun throughout recess. Ben thanked Bright for that idea and for being fair.

Rather than let this spoil their friendship, they solved the problem well. The lesson? Let's find out.

When You Do Not Agree with a Friend

- **Take a deep breath and try to be calm:** You cannot talk, think, and act well when angry.

- **Talk and listen:** You should share your part. Sarah wants to play with a toy. Jack says he wants to play because that is his favorite toy.

- **Understand the other person:** Sarah realizes that Jack loves the toy, and Jack finds out that Sarah has not played at all.

- **Find a solution that makes everyone happy:** Sarah and Jack agree that they would take turns for 3 minutes each.

Games to Help Learn Conflict Resolution

- **Role-playing games:** Pretend to be different characters and practice solving problems together.

- **Cooperative board games:** Play games that require teamwork, like "Forbidden Island" or "Pandemic."

When coming up with a solution that everyone loves, speak well to keep your friendship strong.

Your Words, Your Space: How to Politely Stand Your Ground

You need to tell others what you think and how you feel nicely and let them know your limits. To speak your mind politely, you need to speak clearly with a calm and clear voice.

It would help if you also used "I" statements. This means you would need to always start saying what you feel with "I." For example, you can say, "I do not like it when you do not listen to me." Well, each time you talk, tell the truth about your feelings.

To learn how to tell others your thoughts and feelings in a nice way:

- Know what you do not like.

- Say no when you need to. For example, you can say, "I do not like that."

- Stand by your words, but be polite. For instance, you can say, "Thank you, but I do not like to play that game."

Hands-On Activity

Draw a picture of a bubble around yourself. Write or draw things you like and feel good with inside the bubble. Outside the bubble, write or draw things you don't like or that make you feel bad.

Interactive Exercises

- Sit in a circle with friends or family. Take turns sharing your feelings about different situations using "I" statements. For example, "I feel happy when we play together."

- Act out scenarios where someone needs to set boundaries, like saying no to sharing a toy. The group guesses what the boundary is and discusses why it's essential.

- Make a list of activities or situations. (For example, sharing a toy or playing a game.) Each person takes turns saying if they would say "yes" or "no" and why.

- Create opinion cards with different questions or situations. For example, consider these questions:

  - Do you like ice cream?

  - How do you feel about loud noises?

Take turns picking a card and expressing your opinion using "I" statements.

By practicing these activities and exercises, you'll learn how to express your thoughts and politely set boundaries.

Adjusting to Changes: How to Adapt When Things Change

Buddy, things in your life will always be different. For example, Dad and Mom could move to a new house, which could mean that you would start a new school and leave old friends. When these changes occur, it can make you worried or sad.

Don't worry. I'll help out. But first, let's talk about some of the reasons for such changes:

What Can Cause Changes

- **Moving to a new house:** This might mean leaving your old friends and getting used to a new place.

- **Changing schools:** You might miss your old teachers and classmates and feel worried about meeting new ones.

- **Making new friends:** You might need help finding people with the same interests as you.

Skills to Adapt to Change

- **Be positive:** Think about the fun things that can happen because of the change. For example, if you move to a new house, you might have a bigger backyard to play in.

- **Be open:** Be ready to try new things and meet new people. For example, when you start a new school, join an activity to meet new friends.

- **Ask for help:** Talk to a parent, teacher, or friend if you feel unsure or need advice. For example, if you feel worried about making new friends, ask your teacher to introduce you to some friendly classmates.

Story Time

Tyla was moving to a new town because her dad got a new job. She felt sad about leaving her old friends and worried about starting a new school. Her dad told her about the new town, its great park, and its big library. Tyla decided to think about all the fun she could have.

On her first day at the new school, Tyla was shy. She remembered to be open and try new things. When she saw a group of kids playing a game she liked, she asked if she could join. They happily included her, and Tyla made new friends.

Whenever Tyla was unsure about something, she talked to her Dad or teacher. They helped her feel better and gave her good advice. Before long, Tyla loved her new town and school.

When you stay positive and open and ask for help, you can adapt to the changes and find happiness in your new situation.

With this detailed explanation, you are set to make good friends for yourself! But how would you interact when there are many kids whose skin colors are different from yours? You'll find out in the next chapter!

Chapter 4: World of Colors— Valuing Diversity

Imagine if every food tasted, smelled, and looked the same. Tell me, even if it was healthy, would it not be boring? Yes, it would. Our world is so beautiful because we have different colors and tastes. Well, this isn't just about food; it's also about people. We come in many colors, with different eyes, hair, shapes, and sizes. We speak different languages and have different cultures. These differences make us special and beautiful.

Buddy, you can't live your best life if you only see things one way. So, as you connect with people, you need to understand

and value your differences. This is how you get along with others.

This chapter will teach you about the differences that add beauty to our world!

Discovering a Diverse World: Why Differences Are Important

Let me remind you of your box of crayons. Imagine that all the crayons in your box were a single color. Would you be able to make your coloring books beautiful? Of course not. Like crayons, people come in different colors.

The differences in people will help you in three ways:

- **You will learn new things.** You'll learn about new foods, traditions, and games from kids who are different from you. For example, your friend might celebrate a holiday. This will help you learn about their customs and try some delicious sweets!

- **You will make new friends.** Kids from different countries will tell new stories. They will help you see the world differently. It's like a fun adventure that might help you travel the world without leaving your country.

- **You will be kind and respectful.** If your classmate uses sign language, you might learn some signs to talk with them and make them feel okay. It's important to be kind and make everyone feel included.

Some Aspects of Diversity

Here are some aspects of diversity:

- **Race:** This is the color of skin and other physical features of individuals. A person can be Black or White or other colors.

- **Culture:** These are our way of doing things and the food we eat. For example, some people eat sushi, while others love tacos!

- **Religion:** They are the beliefs we follow and the holidays we celebrate. Some people celebrate Christmas or Eid al-Adha, while others celebrate another special holiday.

- **Gender:** This is about being a boy or girl, or someone in between.

- **Disability:** Some people might use a wheelchair, hearing aid, wear glasses, or might need help in different ways.

How to Celebrate Diversity

You can celebrate diversity in two ways:

- **Share and listen:** Share your way of doing things in your country with your friends and listen to theirs.

- **Ask questions:** If your friend wears a special dress for a holiday, ask them about it.

The world is like a rainbow. It's beautiful because of its many colors. It's better if we appreciate our differences. We should celebrate them.

What Makes You Special: Understanding Everyone's Difference

What do you love doing that your friends do not enjoy doing? Write down one or two of those activities. Are you done writing? That's good!

Mack loves drawing, but his best friend prefers playing soccer. Is that the same with you? You may be good at math, while some of your friends or kids at school enjoy reading. Some kids might be good at playing soccer, while others love reading.

The key is that everyone is different. These differences make us special!

The Importance of Respecting Our Differences

Now, we will explain some terms. They will help you understand why differences are good.

- **Personal interests:** Personal interests are simply the things you love to do. These interests could be baking cookies, or they could be building with LEGO bricks. You can have more fun conversations and learn different things. You can also share what you have with others.

- **Abilities:** Abilities are simply what you're good at. For example, you might love solving puzzles (your interest) but might not be good at it (your ability). If Caleb is better at singing than you, it does not mean that Caleb is better than you. It only means that Caleb is just special in his way, just like you.

- **Character traits:** This is simply the way we behave and feel. A kid at school might be funny, while others are kind or brave. These traits make us who we are.

Games to Try

- **Talent show:** Have a mini-talent show with your friends or family. Everyone gets a turn to show something they're good at.

- **Interest swap:** Pair up with a friend and share something you love doing. Teach each other your favorite activity.

- **Kindness bingo:** Make a bingo card with different kind acts, like "give a compliment" or "help a friend." Every week, do what the Kindness Bingo Card suggests.

If you keep understanding and respecting each other's differences, we will make the world more colorful. We will also make it more exciting!

So, the next time you are with a friend, listen to them, be kind, and find humor in your differences.

Thinking Fairly: How to See Past Stereotypes

Stereotypes are unfair ideas about people based on their background or appearance. For example, some say that "boys are good at sports." What they mean is that girls are not. But is that true? No.

A few other stereotypes are, "Girls like pink," "Boys don't cry," "Girls play with dolls," and "Girls are better at reading."

How to Overcome Stereotypes

If you think only boys can play sports or only girls can dance, it can stop a kid from trying either activity. So, if you believe in stereotypes, you might not fully respect or understand others. You might also miss out on making great friends or learning new things.

If you are open and know people for who they really are, you will see their true talents and interests. It is also good to treat others fairly. So, do not judge a book by its cover. Whether you're at school or home, give everyone the chance to display who they are.

Practical Exercises to Solve Stereotypes

- **Mix-and-match games:** Mix-and-match games are a fun activity. Write different hobbies on paper. For example, soccer, drawing, or cooking. Mix them up and pull out two. Think about how anyone, no matter their gender or background, can enjoy these activities.

- **Find the stereotype:** Watch a TV show or read a book and try to find examples of stereotypes. Talk about why these stereotypes aren't good and how the characters could be shown differently.

- **Role reversal:** Pick activities you wouldn't normally choose in a group of friends. Maybe boys can try dancing and girls can play a sport.

How to Think Fairly

- **Ask questions:** When you meet new people, ask about their hobbies and interests. Listen and learn from what they say.

- **Fight stereotypes:** If you hear a stereotype, speak up and say why it's important to see everyone as unique.

- **Be open-minded:** Keep an open mind and be willing to change your thoughts about someone as you get to know them.

Be fair and see past stereotypes. You'll make new friends and learn amazing things about people!

Together We're Stronger: Building a Welcoming World

What would the world look like if everyone were respectful and kind? It would be so nice, right? So, let's talk about what you can do to make everyone feel valued and welcome.

How to Create a Welcoming World

Here are three tips that can help you learn:

- **Be kind and respectful:** Treat everyone with kindness and respect, just like you want to be treated. For example, do not always forget to always say "hello" when you see someone, share with other kids, and listen to what kids at school have to say.

- **Include everyone:** Invite others to join if you love to play a game or engage in other activities.

- **Speak up:** If someone is being treated unfairly, and you know of it, say something. You can tell a teacher or an adult. That does not make you a telltale. It only shows that you care.

Hands-On Activity #1: The Friendship Circle

Let's try this fun activity called "The Friendship Circle"!

- Get a group of friends together.

- Sit in a circle so everyone can see each other.

- Take turns saying something nice about the person next to you. It could be, "I like how you always share your toys," or "You have the best laugh!"

This game helps everyone feel valued and included. It shows everyone has something special to share.

Hands-On Activity #2: Inclusion Poster

- **Create a poster together:** Gather your friends. Make a big poster with a drawing of happy kids playing. Use lots of bright colors.

- **Make it fun:** Indicate what each person on the drawing is doing. For example, add that they share toys, listen to each other, or help someone feeling sad.

3. **Display your poster:** After you finish your poster, hang it where everyone can see it. Put it in your classroom, bedroom, or community center. The poster will spread kindness. It will make sure everyone feels welcome.

Creating a welcoming world will make your home and family stronger. It will make everyone happy.

Even with the differences in the world, you can make good friends and be good friends. The key point is to be respectful, kind, and treat others well. Good lessons so far, aren't they?

Okay, it's time to move up a little bit. This time, you want to learn how to be a big kid—making decisions and solving problems. Are you set? Let's go.

Chapter 5: Decision Heroes— Mastering Problem Solving

One evening after school, Caleb ran to his mom and said, "Mom! I can't find my airplane!" Mom asked, "Where did you last see it?"

Caleb replied, "I don't remember." Mom looked all around, searching high and low. Finally, she found it behind the couch. You already guessed right—Caleb was very happy when she showed him his airplane!

Like Caleb, have you ever needed help from your parents? That's okay. Asking Mom and Dad for help is fine. But imagine how proud Caleb would feel if he found his airplane himself!

Yes, it's cool to do things independently, because you will learn a lot and feel like a superhero.

So, let's learn how to do things yourself in this chapter and feel really good about it!

What Is a Problem? Understanding and Defining Problems

Imagine you're playing football outside with your friends. Suddenly, something you did not expect happened. Your ball got stuck in a tree. What has just happened is what we would call a problem.

Okay, let's get deeper into knowing what a problem really is. Read on to find out more!

What Is a Problem, Really?

In the scene above, a problem is when something does not go the way you planned it, or where you feel stuck or are not sure what to do next. It's like a difficult puzzle you have to figure out.

But how would you know that something is a problem? Let's talk about the three parts of a problem.

Step 1: Knowing When There Is a Problem

The first step is to think about how you feel. If something makes you sad, angry, or confused, that could be a problem. For example, if your favorite toy breaks and you can't play with it anymore, that's a problem, because you really want to play!

Now that you know that there is a problem, the next step is to break it down.

Step 2: Breaking Down a Problem

When there is a problem, it is good to think about why it's happening. For example, if you and your friend cannot decide which game you should play, then ask yourself, "What might be the problem?" Let's think about one: The problem here might be that you both want to play different games. If that is the reason, it's okay! It's common among friends.

Now, let us move to the third part.

Step 3: Solving a Problem

Here comes the fun part—solving the problem! At this stage, you get to use your super brain. You can start to think of different ways to fix things. If it is a game problem, could you take turns finding a new game that everyone will love, or instead, could you think about a different solution? The process of doing that is using your creativity!

This is a good start to the "problem." Remember, everyone has problems, and that's okay. What matters is knowing that there is a problem, breaking it down, and solving it.

How to Solve Problems: Finding the Best Solutions

It is time for you to dive into problem-solving. You will explore some cool ways to find the best solutions and some hands-on activities.

#1: Brainstorming

Brainstorming is when you gather all your ideas together. Think of it like when you gather all your favorite toys in one place. When you brainstorm, you are thinking of lots of different ways to solve a problem or make something fun.

To do that, you can draw, write, or talk about all the cool ideas you have to solve a puzzle or make something nice!

Hands-On Activities

- **Idea Jar**

    - **What you need:** A jar or a box, small pieces of paper, and a pen.

    - **Activity:** Write down different ideas on small pieces of paper and put them in the jar. For example, "Start a DIY craft project with materials that are available at home."

    - **The goal:** When you need to brainstorm, shake the jar and pick out a few ideas to start with.

#2: Breaking it Down

Sometimes, problems can look big, like a big elephant! But breaking them into smaller parts makes them easier to handle. You can solve each part step by step.

Let's take an example: Assume that the problem is a messy room. Sure, it can be difficult to clean it up, but how about we break it down?

For example, you can say

- "I'll start with the toys first."

- "Next, I'll rearrange the books on the shelf."

- "Then, I will vacuum the room."

Did you see, by breaking down the problem, how we found a way around it?

#3: Using Tools

If superheroes use tools, you should use them too. After all, don't you want to be like them when it comes to being able to solve problems yourself? Let's talk about a useful tool to drive home the point.

Mind Maps

- **Materials:** Large paper, markers, or crayons.

- **What to do:** Draw a big circle and let the circle represent the problem. From the circle, start drawing lines out. Write down different ideas or steps that can help solve the problem.

> **Hint:**
> *You can use different colors for different ideas.*

This visual tool will help you keep all your ideas in one place.

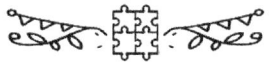

Thinking Smart: How to Be a Problem-Solving Pro

Problem-solving involves thinking like a professional. Professionals are those who have learned something for years and are good at it. Sometimes, doing "mind mapping" is not always enough to solve a problem. It requires something more. So, are you ready? Let's go!

Step 1: Ask Questions

Note: We will use a situation to explain the point throughout this section.

You are faced with this decision: Should you spend your allowance on a toy or save it for something bigger later?

- **What do I know?** "I get a set amount of allowance each week. Toys cost money, and bigger items cost more than my weekly allowance."

- **Is it true or just a guess?** "If I spend my allowance now, I won't have enough for the bigger item later. Saving money lets me buy more expensive things."

- **Where did this idea come from?** "My parents always tell me to save for bigger things. I remember saving up for a special toy before and feeling really happy."

Step 2: Weigh Your Options

- **What choices do I have?** "I can spend my allowance on a toy now or save it."

- **What could happen with each choice?**

  - **Spend now:** "I'll get a new toy right away, but I won't have any money left."

  - **Save for later:** "I won't get a toy today, but I can buy something bigger and better later."

- **Which choice is the best and why?** "Saving seems best because I'll be happier with the bigger item later."

Step 3: Make Reasoned Conclusions

- **What did I learn?** "If I spend my allowance now, I will not have money left for other things. Saving lets me buy bigger items later."

- **What choice makes the most sense?** "Saving my allowance makes the most sense because I really want that bigger item."

- **Why do I think this is the best choice?** "Saving is the best choice because I'll be happier with the bigger item in the long run. I remember how happy I was when I saved up before."

You can make a smart decision about your allowance by thinking through these steps. You can also apply this pattern to other decisions.

Getting Up After a Fall: Turning Mistakes into Lessons

Have you ever lost a game, got a bad grade on a test, or fallen during a race? You are not alone. When these happen, they let you grow and learn. So, let's take a trip to learn how to turn mistakes into lessons.

Before we proceed, it is essential to know that everyone makes mistakes. So, do not feel too bad when you do something wrong.

Now, below are steps to take after making a mistake.

Step 1: Learn from Your Mistakes

When you do something wrong, think about what you can learn.

Here are some examples:

- **If you got a bad grade:** Did you rush through your homework? Next time, take your time.

- **If you lost a game:** Did you lose a game because you didn't practice well? You will need to practice more.

Each mistake is a chance to learn something new.

A Regular Exercise for You

- Create a "Mistake Journal." Write down mistakes you make and what you learned from each one.

Step 2: Stay Positive

It's easy to feel down when things go wrong. But, stay positive by thinking about all you did right and enjoyed.

Here is an example:

- If you lost a soccer game, think about how well you played and the fun you had.

A Regular Exercise for You

- Make a "Good Things" jar. Write down every good thing that happens on a piece of paper and put it in the jar.

- When you feel down, read the notes to remind yourself of the positives.

Step 3: Try Again

Do not give up! If you fall off your bike, get back on and try again. If you don't understand a math problem, keep practicing. Each time you try again, you get a little better and braver.

Someone to imitate:

- Thomas Edison failed many times before inventing the light bulb. He kept trying and finally succeeded.

A Regular Exercise for You

- Pick something you find hard and practice it every day for a week.

- Track your progress and see how much you have improved.

> **Hint:**
>
> *Ask your parents to tell you the story of Thomas Edison.*

Asking for Help: It's Okay to Reach Out

Buddy, the smartest person sometimes needs help. It's true. When you ask for help, it can make your problem much easier.

Why Seeking Help Is Important

Everybody needs help, and that's fine. If you are stuck on a math problem, having trouble with a friend, or feeling sad, ask for help. It can make things better.

> **Consider this:**
>
> *If you're struggling with your homework, ask your teacher. Or, ask a parent to help you understand it better.*

An Activity

Think of a time when you needed help. Draw a picture of the person who helped you and write what they did to help. This will be a constant reminder. You should always ask for help when things are very hard.

How to Identify People You Trust for Support

When you need help, knowing who you can trust is important. Those you can trust care about you and want to help you. They will listen to you and give good advice. You can trust them for advice. They can be your parents, teachers, or older siblings. They can also be your close friends.

An Activity

- Make a "Trustworthy Helpers" list.

- Write down the names of people you trust and can go to when you need help.

How You Can Reach Out for Help

Here are some examples to follow when you need to ask for help.

The Situation: *You have a problem with math.*

Step 1: Know why you need help.

- **The Problem:** "I do not understand this math problem."

Step 2: Choose someone you can talk to.

- **The Search:** "I'll speak with my teacher."

Step 3: Be clear about your problem and ask politely.

- **What to say:** "Excuse me, can you help me with this math problem? I have trouble understanding it."

When you ask for help, it shows you're strong and smart enough to know when you need support.

Hands-On Activities

- **Role-play:** Asking for help from a friend or family member.

    - Practice how you would ask for help with different problems, like homework or needing advice.

- **Number of times:** Do this weekly; you will be good at the art.

You've got this, superstar!

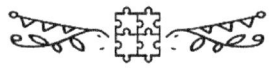

Making Decisions Work: How to Know If You've Solved the Problem

Let us use the messy room from before for the explanation here.

So, when you have a problem, like a messy room or a fight with a friend, you need to find a way to fix it.

Then, after picking the solution, you'll need to find out if it really worked. So, let us look for ways to check if the solution worked.

#1: Try Out Your Solution

First, you will need to try the idea you picked.

When it comes to a messy room, your solution is to clean up. So, give the solution a try. Put the toys in the boxes, keep the books back on the shelf, and get the clothes in the closet.

#2: Look at What Happened

Now that you have tried the solution, take a look at what happened.

Let's go back to your room. Think: "Is my room clean now?"

#3: Ask Yourself More Questions

Think about questions like:

- Did the solution fix the problem?

- How do I feel now?

- How do others feel?

If your room is now clean, and you feel happy and proud, what does that mean? It means that the solution worked!

#4: Learn from What You Did

Sometimes, the solution you pick might not work perfectly. That's okay! You can learn from it.

If you are searching for your toy and you still haven't found it, can you search for it in a different place?

#5: Try Again if Needed

If your first solution didn't work, think of a new idea and try again.

Is your room still messy? Ask a parent for tips on how to organize better.

Solving problems is like doing a puzzle. It might take a few tries, but each time you learn something new, you get better at it! Remember, anybody can make mistakes.

Yes! You are now a decision hero! What's next? Let's see how you can put this lesson into use when you meet a bully.

Chapter 6: Bully Busters— Overcoming Bullying

Do you have siblings or friends who tease you in a fun and friendly way? Those moments can be super exciting and make you laugh a lot! But sometimes, teasing can turn mean and hurtful if it keeps happening. When it gets to that point, it's no longer fun—it's bullying. But guess what? You can stop it without throwing a single punch!

If you're dealing with bullying or want to be ready for it, this chapter is for you! Mind you, mean teasing is just one type of bullying. In this chapter, you'll learn all the different kinds of bullying and how to beat them like a superhero.

Ready to become a bully-busting champ? Let's go!

What Bullying Looks Like: Recognizing Mean Behavior

Let's start with a simple explanation of what bullying really is.

What Is Bullying?

Bullying is when someone or a group of people repeatedly hurts or picks on another person on purpose. This behavior makes the victim feel very upset and sad.

Forms of Bullying

Let's explore the ways bullying can happen:

- **Physical bullying:** Physical bullying happens when someone hurts your body. If a child at school pushes you every day during recess, that is physical bullying.

- **Verbal Bullying:** Verbal bullying happens when someone says mean things. When friends at school call you names like "ugly" or "stupid," yell at you, or make fun of you, they are bullying you verbally.

- **Social Bullying:** It happens when someone hurts another person's feelings by spreading rumors. If some kids at school say mean things behind your back or tell others not to play with you, that is a social bully.

- **Cyberbullying:** This bullying happens online. For example, when a person sends mean messages, posts hurtful things about a person, or shares uncomfortable photos, they are engaging in cyberbullying.

How You Can Recognize a Bully

You can spot a bully, and it's not even hard. Let's find out how!

- **Mean words:** Bullies usually say hurtful words, tease in a painful way, and call others names.

- **Take things:** A bully can take away your snacks, toys, or other items that belong to you.

- **Repeated action:** When a bully says something mean to you, they might keep doing it over and over.

- **Physical Harm:** Bullies can hit, push, or do something to hurt you.

Why Do Some Kids Bully?

Here are three reasons why some people might bully others:

- They want to be in control or feel powerful.

- They are unhappy or dealing with some problems.

- They want to be popular or be part of a popular group.

Impact of Bullying

Bullying hurts everyone involved:

- **Victims:** They might feel scared to go to school or be around some people, lose interest in activities they used to love and enjoy, and feel lonely all the time.

- **Bullies:** They might get into trouble with their parents or at school. It can also be hard for them to find real friends.

Saying "Stop": How to Stand Up to Bullies

Okay, you now understand what a bully is and how you can spot it, but what's next? How to stop it! Standing up to a bully might not be a walk in the park, but you can do it.

So, let's talk about the strategies that work like magic in this section.

How to Stop a Bully

Here are some effective ways to protect yourself from a bully.

#1: Say "Stop" Confidently

If someone is being mean to you, look in their eyes and say, "Stop!" Make sure it is in a clear and strong voice. For instance, if a bully tries to take your snacks or toy, look at them and clearly say, "Stop! That snack is mine!"

#2: Be Calm

It is the goal of a bully to upset you. Therefore, when a bully upsets you, don't show it. Just stay calm and don't show that you are upset. Here's an example: If a bully calls your names, first take a deep breath. It will help you stay calm and not get angry.

#3: Walk Away

Sometimes, saying "stop" might not be enough. So, it might be best to just walk away! For example: During recess, if a bully keeps bothering you, go to your teacher or be with your friends.

#4: Tell an Adult

Always speak with your parents, teacher, or a trusted person about what is happening to you. Max, for example, was constantly being bullied, so he told his teacher, "Bright keeps making me feel sad and calls me names." The teacher then helped Max.

#5: Be with Your Friends

Some bullies are too shy to pick on you when you are not lonely. So, during recess, do not play alone. Play with other people.

Remember: *When you spot a lonely friend, offer to play with them.*

A Game to Practice

What you need: 2–3 persons

Where to find: They can be a friend or family member

What to do:

- One person pretends to be a bully. Then, other people practice all the five strategies mentioned above. (Try them one after the other.)

- After a few rounds, then you can switch roles to allow other people practice too.

Finding Help: Who to Talk to When You're Upset

Do you still remember that our goal is not to beat a bully with a punch? Good!

So, what we want to learn now is how to get help from others, because you cannot beat a bully alone!

Where to Find Help

When a bully upset you, here are four types of people you can turn to:

- **Teachers:** Your teachers can help you stop the bullying and keep you safe at school.

- **Parents:** Mom and Dad will give you support and advice. They can also help you talk to the school if there is a need for it.

- **Other Adults:** They can be your family member or school counselor.

- **Friends:** Your friends at school or at home can help stop you from being lonely.

The "Help Tag" Game

What you need: A group of family and friends; about 3–4 persons

How to Play:

- One person is "It" (the chaser) and tries to tag other people.

- If the chaser is about to tag you, find your way to a safe person (a "helper").

- When you get there, ask for help by saying: "Can you help me?"

- The helper will respond with "Yes!" And then give you a high-five.

- For a few seconds, you are safe in the zone, until you have to run again.

Peter's Story

Jordan was mean to Peter every day at recess and he was feeling sad about it. Jordan usually pushed Peter and called him names. So, Peter did not know what to do and always felt alone.

One day, he decided to talk to Ms. Carter. He explained everything about Jordan's bullying. Ms. Carter carefully listened and appreciated how Peter told him everything. Ms. Carter promised to help him.

Right away, Ms. Carter called Jordan and told him why bullying was wrong. She even spoke with Jordan's parents so that Jordan would not repeat that again.

With what result?

Jordan told Peter that he was sorry.

Peter was so happy that he talked to Ms. Carter.

The lesson: Ask for help when someone tries to bully you. It will make things better!

Remember, if a person is being mean to you, find a friend or trusted adult to talk to.

Feeling Better: How to Heal After Being Bullied

When bullied, you can be sad, and it can hurt. But guess what? You can feel better after. Let us explore some fun things you should do.

#1: Speak with Someone

Tell someone about how you feel. You can start with your parents, friends, or your teacher. How will they help you?

They will

- give you a big hug.
- calm you down with good words.
- cheer you up.
- listen to you.

This is how you can start the talk with anyone. Let's imagine that you are meeting your parents. You can say, "Dad, can I talk to you about what happened at school today?"

#2: Do What You Love

List the things you do that make you happy. For example:

- favorite games
- fun book

- outdoor play

If you perform these or something else, it will make you feel good or even help you forget about what happened.

#3: Remember How Amazing You Are

Are you a kind friend? Are you great at drawing? Do you make people laugh? If you answer yes to one or more of the questions, write them down. Then, anytime you are down, read them. They will give you a boost.

For example, you can write:

- "I am respectful."

- "I am good at board games."

- "I am good at math."

#4: Draw or Write Your Feelings

It might be nice to draw pictures or write your feelings in a journal. For example, you can draw how a superhero (you) beat a bully.

You can also write about happy thoughts and dreams.

#5: Find More Friends

With new friends, you can feel safe and happy. Where can you find new friends?

- playing sports with kids

- joining a club

- finding kids that enjoy the same activities as you

Hands-On Activities

Nature Walk

- **Nature Hunt:** Go on a gentle walk in your garden and look for varying animals, plants, and cool rocks. In fact, you can make a list of what to find, like a pretty flower or a red leaf.

- **Collect and Create:** Gather flowers, leaves, and stones and use them to make a nature collage at home.

Gardening

- **Plant a Seed:** You can plant vegetables or flowers in a pot. Every day, water it and watch its growth. As you care for the plant, you will find it rewarding.

Staying Strong: Building Confidence to Face Bullying

So, superhero, here is the final part of beating a bully with style.

Power-Up 1: Do Not Forget Your Calm Breath

Anytime someone says something hurtful or mean, take a deep breath, hold it for 3–4 seconds, and then blow it out slowly. In fact, you can also imagine an invisible bubble all around you, letting those hurtful words bounce right off it. This will help you think well and stay calm.

Power-Up 2: The Feelings Radar

You should be able to know how you feel. For example, if you are feeling sad, scared, or angry, talk to someone. If you can understand your feelings, it means you have a feelings detector.

Power-Up 3: The Friendship Squad

Heroes do not move alone. They have a squad. So, your squad can be your pet, friends, teachers, and parents. Their goal is to give advice, remind you, or cheer you up.

Power-Up 4: Stay Confident

Be sure to stand like a hero. You can do that by standing tall and putting your hands on your hips. Then, look straight ahead. This is what builds your boldness. When bullies see that you are bold, it will scare them, and they will run away.

Power-Up 5: Take Action

Every superhero deserves a plan! Therefore, before a bully ever reaches you, think about what you can do. You have many options. For example, you can

- tell a friend or older adult.

- walk away.

- calm your breath.

When practicing this daily, you will be ready for a bully.

Linda's Story

Linda, a kid like you, was bullied by Rose. This made Linda feel bad. One day, at recess, Rose said, "You're an ugly little girl." Linda immediately took a deep breath.

Linda now thought about her unique abilities. Then she told Rose, "I know who I am. And I am very proud of myself." She added, "I understand that you do not know what real beauty is."

Rose was shocked. She walked away because the mean words did not get to Linda.

These are all you need to beat a bully without getting physical! Remember to always take a deep breath, respond boldly, walk away, or seek help when necessary.

Trust me, you've got this, superhero!

You're still enjoying the ride, right? Let's talk about one fine skill that will help you stay focused and enjoy this adventure you have started. Meet me in the next chapter!

Chapter 7: Willpower Quest— Secrets of Self-Discipline

Ryan is great at starting his homework. But guess what? He always loses focus because of his toys and TV. Lily is a little different. She talks when her teacher is talking, stands up from her seat even when her teacher has not asked her to, and talks when it is not her turn.

Buddy, what do you think Ryan and Lily have in common? Here is the secret: They both have to work on "self-discipline." I know what you are thinking: "What exactly is self-discipline?"

It's simple: Self-discipline is when you find it hard to control your actions and feelings! You can think of self-discipline as a superpower that helps you focus and do what is right even when it is difficult. So, the focus of this chapter (and I promise not to lose focus like Ryan and Lily) is to help you learn self-discipline in a fun and simple way.

Learning Self-Discipline: The Secret to Getting Things Done

Self-discipline can help you do a bunch of cool stuff and have fun. So, let's dig a little deeper into what self-discipline really is.

What Is Self-Discipline?

Do you remember when I said earlier that self-discipline is like a superpower? Good! Now, think of it again, this time as having a little coach inside your head. The little coach helps you make good choices and stick to them. Sometimes, it helps you to do something important, even if you don't like to do it. When you start your homework, it is that little coach that helps you finish it before you start to play.

Why Is Self-Discipline Important?

You might think: "Oh, I now know why self-discipline is important." Well, let me tell you more:

- **You will do better at school:** With self-discipline, you can focus more on your studies. Do you know what that means? It means that you'll understand your lessons more and get good grades!

- **You will be able to learn awesome hobbies:** Are there things you want to learn like drawing, playing soccer, playing the piano or guitar? Then, you need self-discipline. It will help you practice regularly and improve your skills.

- **You will help Mom and Dad at home:** Self-discipline will move you to help Mom and Dad with chores, even when they do not ask you. Do you know the result? Mom and Dad will be so proud of you! Don't you want that?

- **You will feel good:** Each time you finish your homework, how do you always feel? Good and proud of yourself, right? That is what will happen to you every day with self-discipline. It is a good feeling!

Try This Fun Challenge

For this week or next, try this self-discipline challenge:

- **Step 1:** Pick an activity you want to be better at. (For example, reading a book chapter daily, learning a new dance move, or learning a musical instrument.)

- **Step 2.** Every day, mark your progress on a sticky note or on a chart.

- **Step 3:** Once the week is over, celebrate what you have been able to do. You can do that with a fun activity or a yummy meal.

$$\ggg \longrightarrow \rightarrow \odot \leftarrow \lll$$

Setting Goals: How to Plan Your Success

Setting goals can help you become more self-disciplined, which will lead to success. Let us now take some time to learn what a goal is.

What Is a Goal?

A goal is something you want to achieve. For example, any of the activities you plan to do in the Fun Challenge is a goal. Goals will give you the direction to go, just like a map!

How to Set Goals You Will Achieve

The steps below will help you set goals you can achieve:

- You can start by thinking about what you want to achieve. For example, do you want to learn how to bake cookies or cook daily? Any activity you pick is your goal.

- Be clear about what you want. It is not okay to say: "I want to play soccer well." Instead, say: "I want to learn how to play soccer for 20 minutes daily."

- Make sure it is something you can actually do. For example, if you have not baked before, do not set a goal to bake a fancy cake.

Good. Now, the next lesson is: How can you achieve the goals you set?

How to Break Down Goals into Manageable Steps

Big goals can seem scary, but breaking them down into smaller steps will make them easier:

- **Write, write, write:** Get a piece of paper and write down your goal.

- **List the steps to take:** For instance, if baking cookies is your goal, your steps could be:

    - **Step 1:** Find the recipe.

    - **Step 2:** Gather the ingredients you will need.

    - **Step 3:** Follow the recipe so you can make the dough.

    - **Step 4:** Bake the cookies.

- **Do it bit by bit:** Do not try to do everything at once. After you complete a task, pause and reset.

Why You Should Keep Trying

Sometimes, it may be hard to reach your goal. When that happens, you need to keep trying. When you keep trying, you will be able to stick to your goal. Let me tell you this secret: Every big achievement you see or hear of takes lots of time and effort.

Managing Your Time: Tips for Doing More in Less Time

Now, it is *time* to talk about *time*. (Lol!) Do you know why it is good to learn about time? It is part of being self-disciplined. Also, when you manage time well, you will be able to complete your chores faster and do more fun stuff.

So, time management is a skill you really need!

How You Can Manage Time Well

- **Start with a to-do list:** This means that you have to write everything you want to do. Then, as you finish each activity, mark it. When your list gets shorter, it will make you feel great.

- **Pick tasks that are more important:** It is good to start with tasks you find more important. Playing with your toys and doing your homework is fine. But which is more important? Your homework. So, before you play with your toys, finish your homework.

- **Use a timer:** Set a timer for each assignment you do. If you have a 10-minute window for your homework, program the timer. Once the duration expires, take a moment to relax. After the short break, you can pick another task.

- **Plan each day:** Before you start each day, write what you want to do for that day. This will allow you to know what is next instead of thinking hard about it.

- **Do not put things off:** Waiting until the last minute before you do something is not nice. As soon as possible, start your tasks. This will prevent you from rushing and not doing a good job. If you put off reading for tests until the last minute, you might not read well and get a poor grade.

Practical Example

Let us imagine that you have these three tasks:

- You want to draw a picture.

- You have homework.

- You have household chores.

Do these:

- **List:** You can list them.

- **Arrange:** Arrange in order of importance. For example, it can be: Homework first, house chores next, then, finally, drawing.

- **Set a Timer:** You can say to yourself, "I will spend 25 minutes on my homework, and 15 minutes on house chores, then I can spend as much time as possible on my drawing."

Staying Sharp: How to Focus and Pay Attention

So now, let's talk about focus!

Focus is like wearing glasses that help you see things better. When you wear these glasses, it may take time to look at things clearly. So, how can you improve your focus? Let's find out!

How to Boost Focus

You can build focus by doing this:

- **Get a super space:** This space should be quiet and comfortable. This space must be free from distractions like toys or loud noises. Also, the space can be your table or your room.

- **Break it down:** Break down big tasks into smaller parts. For example, if your teacher gave you a project, divide it into sections like:

- ○ researching

- ○ writing down

- ○ doing it

- ○ Make sure you complete one part at a time!

- **Use the 5-minute rule:** This means setting a timer to focus on what you are doing for 5 minutes without looking at something else. Once the timer rings, take a break.

- **Play games:** There are many focus games you can try. For example, try memory games or puzzle games.

> **Hint:**
> *Ask your parents for a good focus game that is exciting and fun.*

- **Get involved in mindfulness:** Mindfulness means paying attention to something that is happening at the moment.

> **Try this:**
> *Focus on your breathing for 5 minutes. Notice how you breathe.*

A Practical Example

If you want to complete a puzzle, do not do all the puzzles all at once. Start by completing a section at a time. Set a five-minute timer to focus on a part of the puzzle for five minutes. Once the five minutes is over, take a break. Repeat until you finish your tasks.

A Focus Challenge

- Pick one task of your choice. (Try reading and drawing for a start.)

- Find a special focus space.

- Set a timer for 10 minutes. For those 10 minutes, make sure you concentrate on those tasks.

- Once you complete the tasks, check how much you enjoyed that focused time.

With continuous practice and fun, you will learn to be more focused.

Building Good Habits: The Power of Doing a Little Bit Every Day

Has it ever occurred that after playing with your toy one day, you left it on the floor without returning the toy to its bag? Well, you are not alone. Many kids your age do that, too! Playing with toys and not tidying them up is a bad habit. But let's learn what can help you in building good habits.

How to Build Good Habits

When you do something regularly, it becomes easier and more fun! So, let us learn how to build good habits:

- **Start simple:** Let us say you want to make it a habit to make your bed every day. Start with the pillow. Each time you wake or use the bed, pull up the pillow. Once you start small, you can then move to making the whole bed.

- **Set a routine:** Routines are your-to-day-activities. If you want to read every day, find a special time— maybe before bed. Also, be sure to stick to it. When you do it at the same time every day, you will build that habit.

- **A habit tracker can help:** A fun chart with a sticker on it will help you complete your habit. Let's say you want to brush your teeth twice daily. Put a sticker on a sticky note. Once your chart starts to fill up with stickers, you will be motivated to do more.

- **Ask for help:** You can build a good habit with a family member or friend. Ask them to join you. If you want to learn to draw, for example, you can ask your sibling to join you. That can motivate you.

Hands-On Activities

- **Routine rhyme time:** These activities involve creating a fun rhyme that will help you remember the new habit you want to learn.

If you want to learn to keep toys away, find a song you can sing as you do the task.

> **Hint:**
> You can find songs about keeping toys away on the internet. You can even get creative by composing one for yourself. You can also ask Mom to teach you a rhyme.

Facing Obstacles: How to Overcome Distractions

Distractions are things that can take your attention away from what you are doing or from your goals. It can be as simple as looking somewhere else.

In this section, you will learn common distractions and how you can overcome them.

Types of Distractions and How to Overcome Them

Here are six common distractions and how you can overcome them:

#1: Noisy Environments

- **Likely causes:** Noisy siblings, loud TV sounds.

- **How to overcome:**

  - Select a quiet place.

  - Listen to calming music with your earphones to block out the noise. Of course, do not make it a habit.

#2: Tablet or Phone Notifications

- **Likely causes:** Messages from network providers or notifications from games.

- **How to overcome:**

- Turn off notifications by setting the device to DND (Do not Disturb) mode.

- If you do not need the phone for your homework or for your goal, keep it in the other room or somewhere else.

#3: Messy Room

- **Likely causes:** An unkempt bed, litter, or scattered notebooks can make it difficult to find what you need or stay focused.

- **How to overcome:**

  - Return your notes to their rightful places immediately after each assignment

  - Keep toys in their lockers once you are done.

  - Clean the space before starting any activity.

#4: Feeling Thirsty or Hungry

- **Likely causes:** You are far from home, or your mom or dad may not be done cooking.

- **How to overcome:**

  - Keep healthy snacks and water close.

  - Eat and drink before you start to work on your homework or something else.

#5: Fun Games or Toys

- **Likely causes:** Games and toys are tempting.

- **How to overcome:**

  - Set aside some playtime so you can focus on what you are doing.

  - Use a timer. When the timer goes off, move on to other tasks.

#6: Feeling Bored or Tired

- **Likely cause:** Tiredness or uninteresting activities.

- **How to overcome:**

  - Schedule breaks so you can rest and start again.

  - You can switch to a different task if your homework is boring. After the first timer is over, switch to another activity. Once the timer for that activity is over, return to the original task.

There you go! Did I lose focus? No. So, it is your turn to start practicing self-discipline. Do well in practicing all the tasks in this section.

We talked a lot about *home* in this section, no? So, let's go home. This time, you will be learning how you can master home responsibilities.

Chapter 8: Independent Explorers—Mastering Home Responsibilities

Wow! You have a comfortable bed to sleep in, yummy food to eat, cool clothes to wear, fun toys to play with, and shoes for your adventures. All these awesome things make your home super special, right? All thanks to Mom and Dad, who have worked really hard to give you these wonderful things!

But here is the sweetest part: You can help Mom and Dad, too! Yes, you can be a big helper around the house. How? By doing some simple chores and duties. Don't you want to be a champion for your family? So, in this chapter, you'll learn how to be a fantastic helper with household chores, ready to do any task with a smile!

The Path to Independence: First Steps to Doing Things on Your Own

Independence may sound like a big word, but it simply means "doing things on your own." You're quite impressive if you can manage tasks by yourself and succeed. Let's explore what independence really means.

What's Independence?

Being independent is not just about cleaning your room or making your bed—of course, these tasks are super important. The full meaning is being able to care for yourself and feel proud of the things you can do. Let's start with housework.

Housework Is a Big Deal

Housework is not just a bunch of chores. When you help at home, you will learn many skills that will help you become more independent.

We will now use one house chore to show the skills you can learn.

Our Task: Making The Bed Daily

The Goal: Make your bed every day or each time you wake up from it.

Lessons:

- **You learn to be responsible.** When you make your bed, you are learning to care for your space and keep your room clean. It is like being the boss of your room!

- **It teaches you daily routines:** When you do it every day, you will get used to it. This will make you more organized.

- **It makes you feel good:** Each time you make your bed, you will feel super proud of yourself. That small win will make you feel great and push you to do more cool things.

- **You learn to pay attention:** When you arrange your pillows and smooth out your blanket, you learn to pay attention to details and do things carefully.

Four fine lessons to learn from making your bed alone. And let me tell you something: There are countless more lessons you can learn from making the bed.

Your Task

Are you ready for your first independent mission?

> **Task:**
>
> *For a full week, volunteer to set the table for dinner.*
> *Each time you do, keep a journal to* **write how you**
> **feel** *and* **the lesson** *you are learning.*

My Space, My Responsibility: Keeping Things Tidy

Your space is like a special zone. It can be your room, homework desk, or a cool little corner where you keep your favorite books and toys. We all have a space; it does not matter how big or small our house looks.

But did you know that having space means that you have a responsibility to keep it tidy?

We will now learn the importance of tidying and managing your space.

Why Should You Tidy Your Space?

Think of your space as a kingdom. Each time you keep it clean, you ensure your kingdom stays happy and shiny. But there is also another plus: You will easily find your favorite toys.

Doing Your Homework

When you do your homework yourself, you will learn and become smarter. Plus, it is your chance to show off your skills.

After reading this chapter, **set up a special spot** in your home where you will always do your homework.

It should be a place to focus—no TV or loud noises.

Learning to Manage Your Stuff

When you manage your stuff, you learn to care for the things you have. For instance, if you return your toys to the right place after playing with them, you are learning to care for what you have. Also, do not leave your notes everywhere in the room after homework. Keep them in the right place.

Tasks for You

- **Set a timer:** Can you race against the clock? Try this: After playing with your toys, set a time frame and see how quickly you can put them back in their spots. Ready, set, go! Do this every time you play with your toys.

- **Homework station:** Prepare a space. Call it your "Homework Station." This space will have all the supplies for doing your homework. Mom and Dad can help with setting up.

- **Daily duties:** Every day, before going to bed, check your space and see what you need to tidy up.

When you learn to keep your space tidy and manage your space, you will feel more organized.

Helping Out at Home: Your First Chores

You can do many special tasks at home to keep it organized and clean. Are you ready? Let's go!

Chores to Do at Home

These cool chores will make you a hero at home and make you Mom and Dad's sweet helper.

- **Sorting the laundry:** Sort clothes into piles by type or color.

- **Organizing your toys:** Put games or toys back in their spots after each play.

- **Setting the table:** Set spoons, forks, and napkins on the table before everyone comes to eat.

- **Sweeping the floor:** Use a broom to sweep dust and crumbs from the floor.

- **Dusting surfaces:** Use a duster or cloth to remove dust from shelves or tables.

A Task for You

Practice these house chores:

- taking out the trash

- meal prep

> **Hint:**
>
> *Ask Mom and Dad for directions on how to do them.*

Chef in Training: Safe and Simple Cooking for Kids

In one of the last tasks, I asked you to learn "Meal Prep" as a chore. In this section, we will talk more about cooking. Yes, I want you to be a little chef.

As we move into the world of cooking, let's talk about kitchen safety first.

Kitchen Safety

You have to learn some safety tips before you start to cook.

- **Hot stoves and ovens:** Stoves and ovens can get very hot. Make sure you ask an adult to help lift them off and on.

- **Sharp knives:** Knives help you cut food. However, you have to be very careful. When it comes to cooking, let an adult do it. If Mom has a special kid-safe knife, ask for it.

- **Spills and messes:** Spills are very likely when cooking in the kitchen. When that happens, wipe it up carefully so it does not result in slips and falls.

Okay, now that we're done with the basics, let's try some cooking!

Simple Cooking

Note: *Try all of these with an adult.*

#1: Make Your Sandwich

- Grab your favorite bread.

- Spread some jam or peanut butter.

- Add some yummy toppings.

Yes, there you go.

#2: Fruit Salad Fun

- Cut up fruits like bananas, apples, and berries into small pieces.

- Mix them in a bowl for a colorful fruit salad.

#3: No-Bake Treats

Ingredients

- 300g digestive biscuits

- 100g caster sugar

- 1 tsp vanilla extract

- 500g full-fat soft cheese

- 300g raspberries

- 300ml double cream

- 100g unsalted butter, melted

- Icing sugar for dusting

Directions

- Use a food processor to turn the biscuits into powder form. Transfer into a bowl and stir in the melted butter to make the mixture look like wet soil. Put the buttery mixture in a tin and press into the base with a spoon to get a smooth, even layer. Allow it to chill until needed.

- Put the soft cheese, vanilla, sugar, and cream in a bowl and beat with an electric whisk till it thickens and becomes creamy. Then, pour the raspberries into the bowl and press some raspberries to squeeze out some of its juice.

- Put the cheesecake mixture on the chilled base and smooth the tip with a spatula.

- Allow it to chill for 6 hours.

- Dust with icing sugar (optional).

- Serve and enjoy later!

Cooking Skills to Learn

Below are some cooking skills to learn:

- **Measuring ingredients:** Learn to use measuring cups and spoons so you can get the right amount of ingredients.

- **Mixing and stirring:** You can stir ingredients together with a spatula or spoon.

- **Following a recipe:** When you are about to cook something different, read the recipe step by step.

Cooking can help you learn new skills. So, in the coming weeks, during the weekend, practice one of the simple dishes. But make sure to wear your apron before you start cooking.

Cleaning Up Dishes and Keeping the Kitchen Tidy

Cooking in the kitchen isn't the only chore that can make you a superstar. Cleaning the dishes and tidying up the kitchen can also do that.

So, little kitchen helper, let us start with dishwashing.

Dishwashing Adventures

Welcome to your dishwashing adventures!

Hand Washing Dishes

Follow these steps if you are washing the dishes with your hands:

- You will have to fill the sink with warm, soapy water. When you get some bubbles—yeah, it's time to work.

- Use a sponge to scrub the dishes clean.

- Lastly, rinse them with fresh water.

- Clean them with a clean cloth and return them to the plate racks.

Your goal: *Keep every cup and plate sparkling clean.*

Using the Dishwasher

Follow these steps if you have a dishwasher at home:

- Place dirty dishes in the dishwasher. Make sure you arrange them nicely and carefully to allow the dishwasher to clean them well.

- Close the door and press the "start" button.

- Watch how the machine does the magic.

- Return clean plates to the plate racks.

> **Fun tip:**
>
> *Think of it as a robot performing a cleaning dance. While the dishwasher is cleaning, prepare the plate racks.*

Now that you have finished the dishes, let's discuss how to keep the kitchen tidy.

Keeping the Kitchen Tidy

You can keep the kitchen tidy with the following points:

- **Wiping down surfaces:** Use a paper towel or a damp cloth to promptly remove crumbs and spills from the countertop after each cooking session. Doing so creates a clean and inviting workspace.

- **Organizing kitchen items:** Put pans, pots, and utensils away in their rightful places. Keep items in their spot.

- **Using kitchen appliances:**

  - **The refrigerator:** Simply open the fridge and check the inside for the ingredients you need.

  - **The toaster:** Put bread slices in the toaster. After, press the button to toast them. When you toast, it's like sending bread on a fun, toasty adventure!

So, kitchen star, cleaning up after cooking will make you a kitchen hero. A clean kitchen can get you ready for a delicious meal.

Keeping Your Space Clean: Sweeping and Vacuuming

Ready to become a super cleaner? Let me tell you about three cool tools that can help you keep your space clean.

#1: Sweeping Like a Pro

Sweeping makes tiny dust and crumbs disappear. Here are the steps to take:

- Grab your broom.

- Stand upright and hold the broom with both hands.

- Now, sweep it back and forth.

> **Try this fun activity:**
> Imagine you're a hero sweeping away the "dusty villains." When you've got a big pile, get all those crumbs and dust bunnies into a pile. Sweep the pile onto the dustpan and throw it in the trash. Yeah, you've saved your space from the messy monsters!

#2: Scrubbing to Make Your Floor Shine

Just like I said, scrubbing makes your floor super shiny. So, get ready to dive into the fun world of scrubbing! Some steps to take:

- Get a mop ready.

- Fill the bucket with soapy water.

- Dip the mop into the bucket and squeeze it.

- Start scrubbing from one corner to the other until you cover the whole area. Do it in a zigzag pattern to spread the soapy water and clean all the spots.

- Fill another bucket with clean water.

- Dip the mop inside.

- Move it around in the water to rinse out the soap.

- Then mop again to remove soap bubbles.

- Once you are done, allow the floor to dry.

#3: The Vacuum Cleaner Adventure

The next tool is the vacuum cleaner. Here are some steps to take to use the vacuum cleaner:

- First, ask Mom, Dad, or your older siblings to help you plug it in.

- Next, hold the handle and push it slowly across the floor. Expect the vacuum to make a fun noise as it takes up the dirt.

Cleaning Tips and Tricks

Here are some tips that can help as you sweep, scrub, and vacuum:

- **Sweep with style:** Sweep in large, sweeping arcs. The cleaner you sweep, the neater your room looks.

- **Scrub in a zigzag pattern:** Move the mop in a zigzag pattern to cover every spot.

- **Vacuum gently:** Move the vacuum gently and slowly.

Laundry Day: Using the Washing Machine

It is now time to learn how to use a washing machine.

Step 1: Gather Laundry

- Gather all dirty clothes. It's like collecting all your treasures together!

- You can use a laundry basket to put all your clothes in.

- Sort them into different piles. For example, let one be for dark colors (red and blue) and one for light colors (yellow and white).

Step 2: Load the Washing Machine

- Open the lid or door of the machine.

- Put the clothes in. Although, you should never stuff it too full. This is because the clothes need space to move and get clean!

Step 3: Add Detergent

Detergents are like magic soap that removes all the stains and dirt. So:

- Pour the detergent into the washing machine drawer (look for its symbol).

- You don't have to pour too much—just follow the instructions.

Step 4: Select the Right Settings

Now, let's pick the right settings for your wash.

- Look for the buttons on the machine to choose the right cycle for the clothes. Most clothes use the "Normal" or "Regular" cycle.

Step 5: Start the Wash

- Press the "Start" button to start the wash.

Of course, the washing machine will make noises when spinning around.

Step 6: Unload and Dry

When it's done, open the lid and take out your clean clothes. Be careful; they might be a bit wet! Next, hang them up to dry or use a dryer.

Note: If you want to use a dryer, follow the instructions and use the right temperature.

Laundry Tips and Tricks

Here are some tips to keep in mind when using the washing machine:

- **Check pockets:** Always check all pockets for any items before loading them into the machine.

- **Don't overload:** Don't add too many clothes.

- **Ask for help:** You can't learn everything all at once, so it's okay if you need help or are unsure about a step.

Yes, laundry champ, go get those dirty clothes clean and shiny!

Little Gardeners: Taking Care of Plants

Do you love to connect with nature? Then, let's learn to care for plants and watch them grow strong and big. In this section, we will examine the simple steps involved.

Starting Small with a Container

If you do not have the space and time, it is good to start here.

Step 1: Planting Seeds

- Get seeds, a small container or pot, and soil. (Plants love to live in the dirt).

- Fill the container with the soil and push it down a little.

- Make a tiny hole in the soil using your finger.

- Then, place the seed inside.

- Cover the seed with more soil.

Step 2: Watering Your Plants

Just like you need water to stay good, plants also need water to grow. Your plants love to drink, so be ready to give water.

- To water your plants, you will need a watering can.

- Give your plants a sprinkle of water.

> **Hint:**
> *A little splash is perfect. If it's sunny outside, give the plants a cool bath and check on them every day.*

Step 3: Sunshine and Fresh Air

Plants love sunshine and air, so, be sure they get plenty of it! This is what you can do:

- Place the pot where it can enjoy the sunlight. It can be on a windowsill or outdoors.

- Take them outside to enjoy a gentle breeze.

Step 4: Checking on Your Plants

Daily, take a look at your plants. This is what you should look for:

- if they are growing new leaves

- if the soil is too wet or dry

You should make sure everything is just right.

More Time and Space? Get a Little Garden

You can make a little garden if you have more time and space. Plant different types of vegetables and flowers. Just remember to do these:

- Water them.

- Give them sunshine.

- Check on them often.

Mom and Dad can get you a fancy watering can, a tiny shovel, and gloves to work in the garden. Remember, when you are done, return the tools to their place and keep the item clean and tidy. Nice! It's time to enjoy your garden adventure!

You have learned a lot! It's time to show that you can do things on your own and for yourself. Although, remember that sometimes you will need help. Do not be shy about asking for it.

As you do all of these, you need to care for your health. How can you do that? Let's learn that in the next chapter.

Chapter 9: Health Is Cool—Secrets of a Healthy Lifestyle

Do you want to feel great and have lots of energy for play and school? If you do, I have a secret: It's all about healthy lifestyles! Being healthy is super cool.

In this chapter, you will learn fun ways to stay active, pick yummy healthy foods, care for your feelings, set up a good daily routine, and even deal with feeling sick. Sounds like a lot? Don't worry! By the end, you'll be happy to learn all the secrets to staying healthy and happy!

The Basics of Staying Healthy: Moving More and Eating Smart

Moving about and eating good food are the basics of physical health. So, in this section, you will learn the importance of exercise—moving about—and eating healthy. Now, let's start with the importance of exercise.

Why Moving More Is Important and Fun

Each time you move your body, you boost your body's energy. This will make your body stronger and happier. Also, your body will work well, and you will have plenty of energy to play with friends, travel, and do new things.

To move around, always

- run around the compound.
- jump like Spider-Man.
- dance to your favorite song.
- play games with friends.

Your heart will beat happily, and your muscles will get stronger to help you have more energy to play.

Fun Idea:

Ride bikes, jump on a big bouncy bed, and play tag with friends. You can do any of these activities after school.

Eating Smart: Sweet and Healthy Foods

Now, it's time to talk about food. Many kids love food. If you are one of them, you will love this part.

Eating healthy or eating smart means only eating foods that are good for you. It's like using the right color for your drawings.

But it does not mean that you will say goodbye to treats. Just do not eat too much. A little bit of cookies and ice cream are good, but here are important foods for you:

- **Fruits and veggies:** They will help you grow and provide you with energy.

Idea:

Eat a rainbow of colors—try red apples, carrots, and green broccoli.

- **Proteins:** They help you build strong muscles to play and carry things. Examples include fish, chicken, and beans.

- **Whole grains:** Foods like whole-wheat bread and brown rice provide long-lasting energy.

- **Dairy:** These are milk, yogurt, and cheese. They are like builders who build your bones.

Moving your body well and eating good food will make you feel great and have lots of energy to play around, learn, and have fun. Also, moving around will help you care for yourself to be healthy and happy.

So, do not stop moving and eat well!

Active Fun: Exploring Sports and Games

Do you know what makes moving around or being active fun? Stay calm; I will tell you here.

In this section, you will learn about games and sports and how to enjoy them.

Fun Sports to Try

- **Soccer:** This is a game where you run around a big field, pass the ball to other people or your friends, and try to get it into the other team's net. When you play ball, you can move around and have fun.

- **Basketball:** Bounce the ball and shoot it to make many baskets. When you play basketball, you will jump, run, and have fun with friends.

- **Swimming:** Swimming involves entering a pool of water and splashing around. When you swim, you will stay fit, can see your muscles, and cool off.

  - *Caution: Only swim in pools for kids and when an adult is there.*

- **Tennis:** Pick a racket and hit the ball back and forth over the net. Tennis helps you learn how to direct your eyes.

Fun Games to Play

- **Hide and seek:** This is when all your friends hide while you search for them. The first person you see will be the next person to find others. This game is fun and teaches you to be quick.

- **Hopscotch:** One person draws a hopscotch board on the ground. Then, players take turns hopping from one number to another. This game allows you to practice balance and jumping.

Daily Exercise Routines

- **Jump rope:** Jump rope for five minutes every day. Pay attention to the number of jumps you can do without stopping.

- **Yoga:** This is simply a calm game in which you pose like a cat or a tree. You can easily do it in your garden or your sitting room.

- **Jogging:** Daily, jog for like 10–15 minutes.

Do It Regularly

Any of these activities does not have to be boring or hard. Daily, do something active, and you will find fun. When you do, you'll feel happier, stronger, and have energy.

> **Hint:**
> *Have healthy snacks or fruits handy when doing those activities.*

Yes! Go out there and have fun!

Eating Well: Choosing Healthy Foods

When you eat healthy, you give your body the fuel to feel great and grow. So, let us learn to choose healthy foods.

Nutrition

Nutrition is all the different things your body needs to stay healthy. It is the superpower that will help you jump, run, and play. When a plate has all the different foods needed to keep the body healthy, it is a balanced diet.

Here are five sections of a balanced diet:

- **Fruits and vegetables:** Fruits and vegetables give vitamins, fibers, and minerals. They help fight colds and are great for the eyes. Examples are carrots, apples, oranges, and spinach.

- **Proteins:** Proteins help repair and build your tissues. Examples are fish, beans, eggs, and chicken.

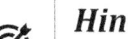

> *Hint:*
> *One weekend, ask Mom for grilled chicken for lunch.*

- **Grains:** You will get energy from grains. They include whole grains like oats, brown rice, and wheat bread.

- **Dairy:** The function is to keep your bones healthy and strong. They include yogurt, milk, and cheese. A glass of milk is fine, and some cheese is great.

- **Fats and oils:** The right fats can help your body and help you get enough energy. Examples are olive oil, nuts, and avocados.

Making Healthy Choices

When choosing what to eat, think about mixing and matching from each section above. Check these:

- **Drink water:** Drink water instead of sugary drinks. Water is super important.

- **Eat different foods:** Try new foods—you might find a new favorite!

- **Portion sizes:** Do not eat too much of a type of food. A few spoonfuls of rice, a small piece of turkey, and a bunch of veggies are great.

Some Examples for Meals

- **Breakfast:** A plate of oatmeal with banana and a cup of milk.

- **Lunch:** Brown rice with cheese, turkey, and cucumber slices.

- **Snack:** A handful of orange slices.

- **Dinner:** Whole wheat bread with steamed broccoli and grilled chicken.

Do not forget that eating well means making the right food choices, enjoying your food, and having fun with what you have before you. You will stay healthy, and your body will thank you!

Happy Mind, Happy Life: Taking Care of Your Feelings

Let's talk about another thing that can make you smile and brighten your day. Want to know what that is? It is your feelings!

Let's start with what a happy mind is.

What's a Happy Mind?

Imagine your mind as a garden. What would you say about a garden full of flowers that enjoy sunshine and rain? Lively and beautiful? Yes! How about a garden full of weeds and many dry spots? It won't be that fun, right? I agree.

It is the same way with a happy mind. A happy mind is like a happy garden. When your mind is happy, it means that you are feeling good.

You Can Keep Your Mind Happy

Keep your mental garden sharp this way.

- **Take deep breaths:** To do this, imagine blowing air inside a big balloon. Take in the air with your nose and blow it out slowly. Each time you are worried, do this to calm down.

- **Do fun relaxation activities:** Draw a cool picture, listen to music you love, or do some yoga poses. These activities will occupy your mind and keep your worries out.

- **Tell others:** What if you have a box where you can keep all your feelings? You will love it, right? Your mom, dad, siblings, and friends are the box you can trust. When you are sad, open the box and tell them how you feel.

- **Think good things only:** Tell yourself only positive things. Instead of saying, "I *won't* pass the test," tell yourself, "I *will* pass the test."

A Fun Game: Feelings Bingo

Goal: Play this game always and anytime you are angry.

How to do it:

- Draw a big square on a box.

- Split each box into four.

- Each square should have different tasks. For example, a box can get, "Tell a joke." Another one can be, "Write a happy note." Another box can have, "Give a compliment," and the last one, "Write a story."

- When you do any of these, tick the square.

- You will get a bingo if you finish all the fun activities in the square.

This way, you can have fun and boost your mood.

Building Healthy Routines: Small Steps for a Better You

Routines are things you do daily that make your day smooth. So, it is good to learn how you can learn a good routine.

What Routines Can Look Like

- **Morning:** What you do each time you wake up—dress for school, eat breakfast, and pack your bag for school.

- **Bedtime routine:** What you do to prepare for bed—brushing your teeth, reading bedtime stories, and wearing pajamas.

Simple Ways to Build Healthy Routines

- **Start small:** Do not do many at a time. Start with one. Then, as you master one, add more.

- **Make it fun:** Use songs, fun charts, or stickers.

- **Be consistent:** Do it daily; you will find it easier.

Some Routine Examples

Below are some examples.

#1: Sleeping Like a Champion

Sleeping is like you are recharging your body. It helps your mind and body stay strong.

Tips:

- **Set a bedtime:** Go to bed at the same time each night.

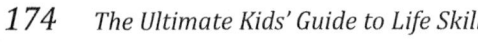

> **Task:**
>
> *The next time you want to sleep, read a storybook to wind down.*

#2: Getting Clean Daily

Getting clean helps you stay fresh and keep germs away. It is also fun to splash around.

Tips:

- **Brush your teeth daily:** This might not be strange to you. But do this twice daily—morning and night.

- **Wash your hands:** Wash before and after meals. Also, wash after playing with your pets or playing outside.

> **Task:**
>
> *The next time you brush, sing or listen to a song while you do it.*

#3: Learn and Grow

If you want to learn and grow, keep your brain sharp. So, what can you do? Let's see.

Tips:

- **Read daily:** Pick a book that interests you and read a little. Do not finish it all at once. Read inside a cozy blanket!

- **Ask questions:** Be ready to ask questions about things you don't know. Keep a journal for learning new things. Every month, think back on what you have learned; it will move you to continue.

Task:

When you are out with Mom or Dad next, ask them a question about what you see. Write the answer in your journal.

Handling Illness: What to Do When You're Sick

Oh no! Sometimes, you can get sick. But don't worry; we will talk about some common sicknesses, how you can avoid them, and the simple ways to handle them.

Common Illnesses

Here are some common illnesses:

- **Cough or runny nose:** A cold can make you cough and lead to a runny nose. When you have a cough or runny nose, do these:

    - Use a tissue to clean and wash your hands after.

    - Use warm tea to soothe your throat.

- **Stomach ache:** Sometimes, eating what your tummy does not like can lead to stomach ache. During a stomach ache:

    - Lie down and rest.

    - Avoid heavy food like fried chicken, white bread, or steak.

    - Drink lots of water.

- **Headache:** It feels like someone is hitting or squeezing your head. It happens when your eyes need a break or when you are tired. When you have a headache:

    - Close your eyes.

    - Rest.

- ○ Avoid screens.

- ○ Drink water.

What You Can Do When You Are Sick

Let us talk about what you can do when you are sick:

- **Rest:** Your body needs rest to fight germs. So, crawl inside a cozy blanket.

- **Drink more water:** Juice, water, or tea can supply your body with more water and make you feel good.

- **Eat only simple meals:** Simple foods like bananas, oatmeal, and eggs are easy to digest and calm your tummy.

Ways to Prevent from Getting Sick

The good news is that you can prevent yourself from getting sick. Follow the steps below:

- **Wash your hands regularly:** This will remove germs that can make you sick.

- **Eat well:** Eat veggies and fruits.

- **Stay active:** Play outside regularly and move around to keep your body healthy.

- **Get more sleep:** Good sleep will help your body fight germs.

Ask for Help

Sometimes, it is good to ask for help when you are sick. Here's who can you talk to:

- **Parents or caregivers:** They will check you, help you visit a doctor, or get you first-aid drugs.

- **See the doctor:** A doctor will confirm your sickness, treat you, and know if you are getting better.

Buddy, take care of yourself whenever you get sick, and soon, you will be ready to play again!

Are you excited that you now know the secrets of healthy living? That's beautiful! But do you know what you can do during an emergency? Well, come with me. I'll tell you that in the next chapter.

Chapter 10: Young Rescuers—Basics of Safety and Emergency

Buddy, let's start with what an emergency is. An emergency is any situation that requires immediate attention. They are like surprise guests that show up when they are not invited. And guess what? They can pop up out of nowhere. But don't worry. Soon, you will become a safety superstar who's ready for anything.

In this chapter, you will learn to be a hero in any emergency. You will learn what you can do to keep yourself safe and sound, keep your home safe, stay safe when you are outside, and how to be safe at school.

So, wear your adventure hat and get ready to be a safety pro!

Staying Safe Everywhere: Learning About Personal Safety

There is something very important about safety that you need to know. That important thing is about staying safe wherever you go.

But why is that important? It will help you enjoy your play without getting injured.

Are you ready? Let's go!

What Is Personal Safety?

Personal safety means caring for yourself and making good choices that will help you stay safe. This involves noticing the dangers or what is happening in your surroundings!

What it Means to be Aware of Your Surroundings

Think of yourself as a detective. Do you remember what detectives do? Yes, they always check for things. You, too, can do that, but with a different goal.

The reason why you are checking is to be safe. So, this is what you should do:

- **Look around:** Pay attention to where you are and try to understand what is happening around you. Check for noises, many people, or sharp objects.

- **Be close to trusted adults:** Anytime you are out, stay close to your parents, older siblings, teachers, or other grown-ups. See these individuals as your safety guide. Do not always stay alone.

- **Be careful when crossing the road:** You will need to look left and right and look left again. That way, you will make sure no cars are coming when it's time to cross.

The Rules of Safe Behavior

- **Stay aware:** Always try to know the things happening around you.

- **Listen and follow the rules:** Listen to safety rules anywhere you are, whether at school, outside, or at home. They will keep you out of danger.

- **Ask for help:** Sometimes, you may feel unsafe and do not know what to do, so call for help. Any trusted adult will help you be safe.

- **Wear safety gear:** Whether riding bikes, skateboarding or something else, wear a helmet and elbow and knee pads. These will protect you from injuries.

- **Trust yourself too:** If something is wrong, or makes you scared or unsafe, trust yourself and speak up. Yes, tell an adult.

So, this is a good start. It's time to learn more!

Playing Safe: How to Avoid Getting Hurt

Do you like sports and games? If so, let's discuss how to avoid getting hurt while doing those activities.

#1: Wear the Right Gear

Before you get set for playing, make sure you are wearing the right gear.

Hints

- **Biking:** Wear a helmet to protect your head if you fall off the bike, and use knee and elbow pads to protect you from scrapes.

- **Soccer:** Wear shin guards to keep your legs from bumps and kicks.

#2: Stretch and Warm-Up

Just like a car that needs to warm up before moving, warm up before you start to play.

Hints

- **Before soccer:** Jog and stretch your legs to prepare your muscles for that activity.

- **Before you dance:** Start with some silly dance moves. This will help you loosen your legs and arms.

#3: Hold on to the Rules

All games have rules, so read and follow them.

Hints

- **Tag:** The rules of the tag are to avoid pushing others and run safely.

- **Basketball:** Follow the rules about dribbling. Also, do not push others.

#4: Be Alert and Focused

Whatever game you are playing, keep your eyes on the game and watch the environment you are running.

Hints

- **Soccer:** To prevent collisions during a soccer match, remain alert and keep your eyes on the game.

- **Tag:** Watch out for other players. Be alert so that you can dodge.

#5: Take Breaks

Breaks are important each time you play.

Hints

- **When playing soccer:** Eat snacks to recharge or take a water break.

- **After intense gameplay:** Stretch your muscles to prevent stiffness and improve blood flow.

#6: Ask People for Help

Are you not sure of what to do during an emergency? Ask questions!

Hints

- **A new sport:** If you have not played a game before, ask the coach or an adult about how to play the game safely.

- **Skating:** Ask for tips on how to stop and avoid falls safely.

#7: Hear What Your Body Is Saying

You can get tired after playing for a while. When that happens, what should you do? It's fine and okay to stop and rest.

Hints

- **After running:** If you feel tired, take a break to recharge.

- **Playing games:** Sit out a bit if you feel pains or aches.

Safe at Home: Tips to Keep You and Your Family Safe

Now, let's talk about how to keep yourself safe at home.

#1: Fire Safety

Fire is good for many things but can also be dangerous. You can be safe around fire this way:

- **Use the kitchen well:** When you are in the kitchen, move away from anything hot. Do not touch hot items with your hands. Use gloves or a cloth instead.

- **Listen to the smoke alarm:** Does your home have an alarm system that alerts the family when there is smoke? Then, when you hear the sound, quickly stand up from where you are and join others in a safe, designated meeting spot outside, such as the front yard or the nearest tree.

- **Listen and obey:** Dad and Mom can tell you something special about what you can do when there is a fire. Listen and obey.

#2: Home Safety

While you work hard to keep yourself safe, you must also keep others safe. So, learn to do these:

- **Lock windows and doors:** When not using them, lock them to keep the home secure.

- **Do not touch any electrical outlets:** An electrical outlet is a spot on the wall where we plug electrical items. Use them carefully and for their intended purpose. Do not stick foreign objects in them; it can be dangerous to your life.

#3: Keep Playtime at Home Safe

You play more at home than in school. So, what can you do to be safe when playing at home?

- **Games and toys:** Handle your toys carefully so they do not break. If your toy is broken, throw it away. Do not play with toys or games that have missing pieces or sharp edges.

- **Keep play area safe:** The play area of your home should be safe. Let it be free from sharp furniture edges or water spills.

#4: During Emergencies

What if there is an emergency? There is a lot you can do. Let's find out:

- **Know the number to dial:** Ask Mom and Dad to teach you how to call 911. Learn your home address, and make sure you know your parents' phone numbers by heart.

- **Know the family meeting spot:** Ask Mom and Dad about a place you can gather in an emergency. When anything happens, run there.

Being Safe Outside: How to Stay Safe on the Street and in Public Places

Safety champ, it is time to learn how to be safe while exploring the world!

Just a friendly reminder: Are you learning this with your favorite juice? If not, ask Mom for a cup! All set? Let us go!

When on the Road

When you are walking outside, keep these in mind:

- **Stay on the sidewalk:** When you walk outside, use the sidewalk.

- **Look both ways:** Before you cross the road, stop, look left and right, then look left again to be sure no car is coming before you cross.

- **Walk on the sidewalk:** Do not run on the sidewalk. Yes, walk like a king.

- **Use crosswalks:** These special spots on the road allow people to cross safely. So, use them.

- **Use signals:** Check for a green walk signal before you cross.

- **Hold hands:** You don't want to feel like a baby, but let me tell you something: It's cool to be a baby. So, hold Mom's hand before you cross.

When Using Public Transportation

Public transportation is the buses and trains you use when going to school or other places. While they are fun to use, safety is key. Below are instructions on how to stay safe while using public transport:

- **Walk in quietly:** When the bus arrives, don't rush in. Go in calmly to avoid falling.

- **Stay calm on the bus:** Even if other students are running around, don't join them. Sit steady. You might even use that time to read your favorite story or talk with a friend.

Avoid Strangers

There are people you do not know outside. So, you need to be careful so you can be safe:

- **Stay near an adult:** Always stay near someone you know and trust each time you are outside. Do not leave the adult to play with a stranger, as this can be unsafe.

- **Call for help:** Call loudly for help or approach another adult (vendor, city worker, passerby) if a stranger is persistent.

- **"No thanks!":** When strangers offer you candy or something else, it's fine to say, "No thanks!" and then walk away.

Watch Your Items

You do not want your items to get lost. Do you? Thus, do these:

- **Keep your bag close:** Keep backpacks or toys close so that someone does not take them away.

There you have it!

School Safety: How to Be Safe at School

You should be safe and happy when you are in this school. It's not hard. So, learn how you can do that:

- **Know the rules of your school:** Learn the school rules you need to follow to stay safe. Rules are created for a reason—to prevent something bad from happening or from it happening again. Therefore, when your teacher gives instructions, listen and obey. It will protect you. Ask Mom and Dad if there are other things you need to know.

- **Stay in a supervised area:** Do not walk about. Stay in an area supervised by other adults. Stay safe!

- **Play safely in the playground:** You can have great fun. So, stay safe in these ways:

  ○ **Use play items well:** Hold the swing tight and do not push when playing with friends.

- **Take turns:** Do not rush, take turns, and do not play rough.

- **Watch out for friends:** When you show kindness to others, they will want to show kindness to you or others too.

- **Pay attention to safety signs:** There might be signs like "wet floors" or "stop" in the school area. Pay attention to them to avoid accidents.

- **When something is not safe, speak up:** Tell an adult or a teacher when you spot something that is not safe.

- **Know the location of first aid kit:** Get to know where you can find first-aid kits. If you need help with minor injuries, you will quickly reach there.

- **Prepare for poor weather:** Wear thick clothes to keep you warm if the weather is too cold.

- **Strangers are strangers:** Strangers are not friends or family. So, don't accept something for them. Be with a trusted friend or adult!

- **Avoid tripping hazards:** Do not keep personal items just anywhere. For example, keep your lunchboxes and backpacks in their right spot.

- **Do not run in the hallways:** Just like the sidewalk, do not run and always keep to your right side so you won't keep bumping into other kids.

- **Be a buddy:** Being kind and helpful can make everyone happier and safer. Did you spot a lonely friend? Invite them to play with you and ask if they are okay.

First Aid Basics: Fixing Cuts, Scrapes, and More

How can you handle cuts, scrapes, and bumps? That is the goal of this section. But first, let us learn what first aid is.

First Aid

Think of first aid as the first medical care you receive when you get injured. First aid helps you fix small injuries. So, let's learn how to do it.

- **Fixing cuts and scrapes:** Small cuts or scrapes can happen in accidents. So, this is what you should do when they happen:

A. **Wash:** *Before you touch the scrape or cuts, wash your hands with soap and water.*

B. **Clean the wound:** *Wash the injured area with clean water. If you have items labeled as "antiseptic," apply them on the spot, too.*

C. **Stop the bleeding:** *Press a bandage on the cut to stop the bleeding. If it does not stop, tell an adult. (**Note:** Do this only when the bleeding is minor; if it bleeds more heavily, immediately press down on the cut and call an adult for help.)*

D. **Cover it up:** *The moment the spot is clean, put on a clean bandage to keep it clean and free of germs.*

- **If it hurts too much:** Small cuts can sometimes cause you pain. When that happens, tell an adult. They will decide if you need to see a doctor.

- **When it is a bump:** An injury can be a bump. If it happens, then do the following:

    A. **Ice it:** *Place ice on the bump. It will reduce the pain from the bumps. Do that for 15 minutes.*

    B. **Relax:** *You can learn to take it easy and not move around for 10 minutes.*

- **When you should get help:** Tell an adult when a cut is bleeding heavily or looks deep. You should also get help if the bump is painful and swollen. They will know whether you should see a nurse or a doctor. If your classmate or a friend is unconscious because of an injury, roll them onto their side and call an adult for help.

Remember, emergencies can happen at any time. But with these basic first aid tips, you can stay safe and reduce pain. Also, always inform an adult when you cannot stop the bleeding or if the pain is too much.

But that is not all I have to tell you about emergencies. I'll share more with you in the next section.

Ready for Anything: Preparing for Emergencies

You are a super kid, and you can do this! Now, let us cover all you need to know to prepare for emergencies.

Preparing for Fire

This is what you should do:

- **Practice an escape plan:** If you do not have one, tell Mom and Dad to create a plan that tells everyone where they can run to where there is a fire emergency. Draw a map of your house with your parents and mark two places you can go when there is a fire.

> *Activity:*
> *Draw a fire safety poster about your fire escape plan. Paste it somewhere in your room to remind you of what to do.*

Preparing for Earthquakes

Earthquakes usually shake things up. So, this is what you can do to prepare:

- **Find safe spots:** Find a safe spot in your house. It should be away from the windows and under a strong table. You can also find safety near a "load-bearing wall." Make sure you ask Mom and Dad about the load-bearing walls in your house.

> *Activity:*
>
> *With your family, practice dropping down, covering, and running to the safe spot.*

Other Natural Disasters

Storms and floods can happen anytime. This is how you can prepare for any of them:

- **Have an emergency kit:** Keep your emergency kit, which includes water, flashlights, snacks, and a first aid kit, in a safe place.

> *Activity:*
>
> *In the following weeks, prepare your emergency kit. Ask Dad and Mom for items that must be there. Then, put them in a lightweight box or new backpack.*

Keep Practicing

Panicking and not knowing what to do are among our greatest enemies during an emergency. Therefore, the more you practice or train ahead, the better you will be ready and bold to face an emergency.

Keep training for any unpleasant events that usually happen in your area monthly or once every two months.

Monthly Activity

Play a simple game and act out varying emergencies to learn how you can respond to them. Try this next month:

- One person makes a sound in the kitchen that sounds like a fire alarm.

- Everyone runs out of the house.

- The first person who makes it out the door explains the way they took. Use that to analyze the fastest place.

- The goal is to keep practicing. With it, you can prepare for any emergency.

You can do the same with other emergencies.

Calling for Help: How to Use Phones and Other Tools in Emergencies

Hey, do you think only lazy people call for help? No! That is not true. In fact, calling for help shows that you are bold.

Let's start with 911.

Using 911

Sometimes, when you need help immediately, call 911. This is what you should do:

- **You need a phone:** It can be a cell phone or a home phone.

- **Dial 911:** Next, press "9-1-1" on that cell phone or home phone.

- **Speak well:** When a person answers, tell them your name, your address, and what is happening. You can call if a crime is in progress or if there's a fire outbreak or car accident. For example: "Hi, I'm Tony. I stay at Pine Street Lake, and there is a fire in the house."

- **Do not hang up:** Do not hang up until the person asks you to. When they ask questions, listen carefully and answer well.

Activity:

Pretend that there is an emergency, then dial a number (not 911). Take turns. One person answers the call, and another tells what happened.

Other Tools to Use

You can use other tools apart from phones. So, let's explore those tools.

- **Walkie-talkies:** If you have walkie-talkies, use them to communicate with someone close by.

- **Use the emergency alarm:** Press it if you have it at home. Because they make loud noises, you will be able to get people's attention.

> *Activity:*
> *Use the walkie-talkie to practice how to say important things first.*

How to Ready Yourself to Call for Help

When you are prepared, you will be able to speak clearly and get help quickly. So, learn these:

- **Know your contact details:** Know your parent's phone numbers and home address. You will be able to say it easily when you need help.

- **Keep important phone numbers:** Try to memorize important phone numbers such as your parents' numbers, older siblings' numbers, or even 911.

> *Activity:*
>
> *Design a card with your address and important phone numbers next week. Decorate it well and save it in your backpack.*

After Calling for Help

Stay calm after calling and wait for the help to arrive!

These safety and emergency basics will get you ready for any emergency! With this foundation on safety, it is now time to learn about technology!

Yeah, it is also exciting, and I promise you will enjoy learning about technology.

Chapter 11: Digital Heroes— Journey Through the World of Technology

Do you enjoy playing games on your mom's iPad, watching videos on YouTube Kids, or watching cartoons on TV? You're not alone—lots of kids love these too! But did you know we wouldn't have these cool tools without technology? Technology is about using our brains to create awesome things. But while these gadgets are fun, they can have some downsides, too.

In this chapter, you'll embark on an adventure into the world of technology. Ready? Let's dive in and enjoy the fun together!

Discovering the Digital Universe: Basics of the Internet and Devices

Your adventure into the world of technology will start with the digital world.

What Exactly Is the Digital World?

Think of the digital world as a big playground with many gadgets. These gadgets include the internet (where you can find fun videos, games, and awesome websites) and digital devices (like your Mom's iPad). All of these tools let you connect and play with your family and friends. But wait—I mentioned the internet, right? What is it?

What Is the Internet?

The internet is like a very big library that is always open. This library connects millions of computers around the world. It does not have books on shelves. Instead, it has games, lots of information, and videos you can find on mobile phones, computers or tablets. On the internet, you can find so many things.

Some Important Digital Devices

Digital devices are those devices you can find in the digital world playground. They can also be used to enter the big library—the internet. Let's show you some:

- **iPads and tablets:** These super-smart books can show videos, play games, and help you learn new, fun things.

- **Smartphones:** These are very tiny, yet, they are like mini-computers that can be carried in your pocket. Smartphones can be used to talk to friends, take photos, and play games.

- **Computers:** Of course, these are big machines that can do many things at once. You can use them to draw, watch movies, and do homework.

- **Televisions:** TVs are fine for watching your favorite shows and cartoons. Some also connect to the internet for games and videos.

How All Digital Devices Work Together

All these devices connect to that big library to do many amazing things. When you use an iPad, smartphone, computer, or other digital device to play a game, talk to friends, watch videos, or search for information, you are connecting to the Internet.

Safe Surfing: Tips for Using the Internet Wisely

The internet is like a park. It is fun, yet you must follow the rules to stay safe. Let's see how.

Know Where You Want to Go

There are many places you can visit using the Internet. These places are sectioned into two:

- **Websites** are like different rooms in the big library. Some are for games, talking to others, buying, and watching videos, while others are for learning new things.

- **Apps** are special tools that can be used on smartphones, iPad, or tablets. These apps can help you play, learn, or even talk to family and friends.

A Task for You

- Draw a simple big house. Call the house the "internet."

- Ask Mom and Dad to show you some websites you can use for fun or to learn.

- Then, mark out the rooms and write the website's name for each room. For example, you can mark Room 1 as "school website" and mark Room 2 as a "game website."

How to Find Information Safely

Not all information online is correct or safe. So, how would you know which is safe?

- **Trusted websites have a padlock:** Most websites with good information have a padlock that shows that the website is safe. (Ask an adult to show you the padlock.).

- **Ask older adults:** If you do not know whether a website is safe, ask your parents. They will help you find out.

A Task for You

Do this with your parents or guardian present.

- Let an adult find two websites. Make a list of what to check:

    ○ Does it look professional?

    ○ Are there many pop-ups and ads?

    ○ Does the website have a padlock on the address bar?

Stay Private

Would you tell a stranger where you live or your name? If that is the case, do not share personal information like your address, name, photos, or other private details.

A Task for You

- Make a checklist for private information and list out all the things you will not share on the internet. Ask your parents to confirm what else you can add.

- Add flowers and stickers and keep it on your wall. This will remind you of what to always do.

Yes! You are all set!

Tracks You Leave: Understanding Digital Footprints

When you walk in the sand at the beach, you leave footprints that show where you have been. Well, guess what? Each time you use the internet, you leave a footprint. Wondering how that happens? Come with me to hear the gist of it!

Understanding Digital Footprints

The footprints we leave each time we use the internet are called *digital footprints*. It involves everything you do online, like posting photos, playing games, visiting websites, and sending messages. You create digital footprints this way:

- **Photos:** Each time you share a picture of you or your pet, that photo will become part of your digital footprint. Anyone who sees the photos will know that you were there.

- **Comments:** Your comments on a picture, game, or website create a footprint. They show readers that you were there, too.

- **Website visits:** When you visit websites, you leave some information showing that you have been to that website.

But buddy, it is really important to care about your footprint.

Why care? How long do you think your digital footprint can last? The answer: It can last a very long time—sometimes forever. That means that whatever you share will be seen by others for years. It's like having your name on a billboard that many people can see. So, you see, thinking well before you share anything is important.

How to Keep Your Digital Footprint Safe

- **Think well:** Before you post anything online, ask yourself: "Do I want everyone to see it? If yes, then you can post it.

- **Keep your details private:** Do not share your phone number, address, or personal information. Keep them like you would keep a secret.

- **Talk to older people:** If you are unsure whether sharing something is okay, ask your parents or any other trusted adult.

A Fun Activity

Find a piece of paper and draw a big footprint on it. Each time you visit the internet, whatever you do, add a little symbol in the footprint. For example, if you share a photo, draw a camera. Do the same for comments, too.

After a full month, check the footprints you have made.

Guarding Your Secrets: Keeping Your Information Safe

Sometimes, you will have to give some of your personal information to a website you trust. But, if you are not careful, some bad people could steal them from you. It's time to learn how to be a hero when it comes to privacy.

Create a Very Strong Password

How can you create a strong password to keep your information safe? This is what you can do:

Your password should be these:

- letters

- symbols

- numbers

This is an example: *Buddy+guide2024*. ('Buddy' is made up of letters, '+' is a symbol, 'guide' is also made up of letters, and

'2024' is a number.) This password is strong, and it will be very hard for others to guess.

A Task for You

- Write down the names of your favorite numbers, colors, and animals. Mix these up with any symbols.

- After creating a strong password, do not share it with anyone.

Knowing Phishing Attempts

Phishing is when a person tries to deceive you so you can share your secrets with them. So, in this case, they will send you a message so you can share your private information with them. They might send fake messages or emails, claiming to be someone you know. Therefore, do not click on it whenever someone messages you asking for your private information.

Guard Your Private Information

Keep your phone number, address, and name private. Only share them with trusted adults. It is also important to check what others can see of your private information. For example, some websites allow only your friends or family to see your personal details. If you get a message you are not sure about, ask Mom or Dad.

A Task for You

- For this section, try creating a strong password using the idea in this section. Then, ask Mom or Dad if it is strong enough. Create another one and ask Mom and Dad to guess. Give them three tries.

- For a full month, try to identify phishing attempts. Next month, try to find out what is similar to each phishing attempt. That way, you will be able to know more when you see one.

Time Well Spent: Balancing Screen Time and Real-Life

Using digital devices does not mean you should always be on the screen! Oh, yes, that does not make Mom and Dad bad parents. Let's talk more about this.

The 2-Hour Rule

Experts have told moms and dads that kids your age should not spend more than two hours on screens each day (Hanigan, 2024). What does this mean? Screen activities like watching cartoons, playing videos, or doing other screen activities, when combined, must not be more than two hours. So, buddy, if you spend all the two hours on Mom's iPad, once it's time, yes, your time is up! But you can mix it up and keep your body active with outdoor activities.

Exercise #1: Screen Time Tracking

It's time to know how much time you spend on screens for a whole week. So, get a piece of paper and draw seven boxes. Each box will represent one day. At the end of the week, see if you have spent more than two hours each day.

- If you did not spend up to two hours, kudos! Get yourself a candy.

- If not, add some fun activities to limit your screen time.

Exercise #2: Screen-Free Challenge

On weekends—a Saturday or a Sunday—do activities that do not involve the screen at all. For example, you could ride bikes or play games with other family members. Once the weekend is over, try writing down how much fun you had.

Guess what? You might even find out other outdoor activities that are better than spending more time on screens!

Why Balancing Is Good

Would you be happy to eat just one type of meal daily for a week? No! You won't be, and I know that. But how about a plate full of veggies, proteins, fruits, and healthy juice? Will that be fine? Yes!

This is the lesson: Screen time alone will cause you to miss out on real-life adventures and make your life boring and unbalanced. So, keep it mixed—a decent time on screen and having healthy real-life adventures.

Learning Online: Finding Cool Educational Stuff on the Web

We have talked so much about using the internet to have fun—playing games and watching videos. But did you know that the internet is also a place to learn, like a real school? So, let us learn now.

Educational Websites

There are many websites on the Internet where you can go to learn. I will tell you a few: *ABCmouse* and *National Geographic*

Kids. These have fun facts, videos, and games about everything. You can learn about animals and space, dinosaurs and the jungle, and even learn a new language.

A Task for You

- This week, visit either of these sites and learn about two animals. Tell Dad about those animals to see how much you have learned.

- Search for more educational websites by typing *"educational websites online"* on Google.

Learning Apps

Remember we talked about apps earlier? You can get these apps on an "online store." There are learning apps like Prodigy Math and Khan Academy that will help children learn a new language or programming basics. With these apps, learning is fun!

A Task for You

- Once each month, try to learn something from any of these apps.

Virtual Field Trips

You can also enjoy a virtual trip. Websites like Google Earth on your parents' phone allow you to travel to places all over the world. For example, when Tara used Google Earth, she was able to tour the Great Wall of China from her room, travel through the Amazon rainforest, and see the stars at the International Space Station (ISS). You can try that, too!

An Exercise to Try

Try to create a learning map in your journal. Write or draw different places you would want to visit on the internet. The map should include educational websites, virtual field trips, and apps. So, try to explore one of the places on your map each month.

Thanks to the internet, you can learn and discover more fun things. So, it is time for you to explore these learning websites. Happy exploring!

Netiquette: Being Polite and Respectful Online

I love the sound of the word "netiquette," don't you? It's a fancy word. In this section, you will learn how to be a netiquette superstar. Let's go!

What Is Netiquette?

Netiquette is having good manners and being kind. It is like saying 'please' and 'thank you' in the real world. But this time, you are doing it on the internet. So, when you are on the internet to post, share, or do anything else, use good words. The more you do, the happier the internet world will be.

Examples of Netiquette

Here are some examples:

- **Kind words:** Instead of saying, "What a silly idea!" say, "Oh! There is a different idea. Can we try it?"

- **Positive language:** When someone shares their drawings, instead of saying, "That's not better than mine," say, "Wow! I love the color you used. Who taught you that?"

- **Think before clicking:** If you want to post a funny picture or video, ask yourself, "will this hurt my friends, siblings, or others?" It's good to laugh, but it should not make others cry.

- **When you make mistakes:** Sometimes, you might do something that will hurt the other person. When that happens, say "I am sorry."

- **When you play games online:** Say good words. If someone is mean, don't join them. Report or return with kindness.

A Fun Challenge

Next week, write something kind and good about your friend. When you get to school, give it to them and see how that makes them feel.

Here is an idea: You can say something nice about your friend's grade, their drawing, their bag, or just anything they have and love. That way, you will learn to be more kind on the internet. Do this once a month.

> *Hint to stay kind:*
>
> *If you talk to a friend face-to-face, would you want to be rude to them? You would not want to. Remain kind online.*

Words have power. Therefore, for you to be the reason a kid will want to learn or have fun online, always say good things online.

Good Digital Citizenship: The Right Way to Connect and Share Online

You're already a great citizen in your country, but did you know you can also be a fantastic citizen of the internet?

Being a good digital citizen is awesome, and you can learn how to be one right here!

Think Before Clicking

The internet is like a big store where some items are cool and others are not. Of course, before you pick an item into your cart, you have to know if you need it. The same is true of the internet.

Before you share something, you have to think. Many people are not happy about what they have said in the past. But I do not want you to be one of them; I want you to be a good citizen of the internet.

So, before you click share, find out if

- **It is true:** Is the information, story, or website true? Does it come from a trusted website or person?

- **It will hurt someone:** How will it make others feel? If it will make them feel bad, do not click or post it.

- **It will tell your private information:** What you share will be seen later by millions of people. So, learn to think about your personal information before you share.

Share What Makes Others Smile

Each time you share things online, you have a chance to make other people smile. You can do that by

- **Being helpful:** If you see a picture of a pet being cared for, share good comments. If you have done something that helped your pet, tell them.

- **Be kind:** Share comments, pictures, or messages that make others smile. Share what helped you solve your homework or where you got the idea from.

- **Respect everyone:** Since the internet is big, many people have different cultures. Remember what we learned about people of color? Yes, they exist on the internet, too. So, they might say something different from what you know. But be respectful in any case.

So, with this, you will be a good internet citizen!

Facing Cyberbullies: How to Stand Strong and Get Help

Is this your first time hearing "cyberbully?" Think again! You may remember it from chapter six, but we didn't cover it much then. Don't worry; we'll discuss it in detail now.

This is your chance to fully understand cyberbullying and learn how to stand up to it and get help.

How You Can Spot the Bad Guys

Bad guys are everywhere, even on the internet. But they will not write it on their profile. Yet, you can spot them. How? This is how bad guys look like on the internet:

- **Teasing posts:** If someone posts unkind things about others or you on social media.

- **Mean messages:** If a person sends you or others messages that make them feel bad.

- **Exemption:** If a person does not let you be part of the chats or online games.

Be Bold for Others

Sometimes, you may see that others are being bulled. What can you do? Be bold for them! You can do that in these ways:

- **Support them:** Send a kind message that will show them that you care

- **Tell an adult:** Let others help. If they can report the bully, they will help.

What You Can Do About a Mean Message

When someone sends you a mean message, do these:

- **Don't reply:** This will make them stop.

- **Block them:** Most age-appropriate websites have the block feature. Go ahead and use it!

- **Keep your cool:** Cyberbullies want to upset you. They want you to feel like you are not strong. But it's a lie. You are stronger than their words. So, take a break from the phone and relax outdoors or indoors. You can also talk to someone with whom you can share how you feel.

If you apply these, you can be sure that you will be a cyberhero who cyberbullies run away from. Or don't you want that? Go ahead and apply these points.

Tech Tomorrow: Exploring the Future of Technology

We've talked about some amazing things about technology. Well, there are even more exciting tech surprises waiting in your future! I bet you've imagined some cool gadgets. Let's find out if any of your dream gadgets might be coming!

Smart Robots & AI

Just imagine that you have a robot friend who can play your favorite games with you or help you with your homework. Since AI helps machines think and learn like humans, we can expect robots to assist with chores or help doctors in hospitals.

Flying Cars

Would you want to travel through the sky in a flying car? Well, it might be a dream that will come through in the future. In the future, you can expect to see cars that will lift off the ground and fly—how cool is that?

Virtual Reality Adventures

Wear special glasses, and phew—you're in a new world! This is known as virtual reality. In the future, you might be able to travel and explore ancient castles, walk on Mars, and swim with dolphins, all from your room.

Super Smart Schools

Digital learning will experience a big change in the future. Imagine learning math by just playing interactive games or studying history with the help of 3D holograms. With more smart schools in the future, learning will be fun and exciting and help you learn in cool ways!

Final Exercise

The goal is to know how close you are to knowing what will happen in the world of technology in the future:

- Get a small container or box.

- Write down five things you feel technology might do in the future.

- Draw a picture of one of those ideas. What can it do, and what does it look like?

- Put both predictions and drawings in the container. Also, add a fun note to your future self.

- Hide the container in a special place.

- In the next 4–5 years, open and see how close you were to knowing what will happen in the future.

So, there you have it! Don't you think that the future of technology is super exciting? I agree with you! So, keep dreaming big!

Digital hero, it is such an amazing time learning about the digital world! You will be taking another turn into the secrets of successful learning. Are you ready? Kudos to you!

Chapter 12: Learning Navigators— Secrets of Successful Learning

Do you like studying? If you do not, that's okay! Many kids don't always enjoy studying, and they find it tough. But here is some good news: You can learn some cool tricks to make studying easier and more fun.

In this chapter, you will learn how to study better and have more fun while you learn. These tips will help you enjoy your study time even more!

Super Studying Skills: How to Learn Anything Faster

Kids who love reading agree that it is an exciting adventure! Let's see how you can be one of those kids, too.

Set a Study Space

Your study space is your special learning area. It should be a place where you can focus and enjoy yourself. You can do it this way:

- **Get a quiet spot:** It should be quiet, with no TV or loud noises.

> *Idea:*
>
> *A comfy spot at the kitchen table or a nice corner in your room.*

- **Be organized:** Keep the study area neat. Put your notebooks, pencils, and erasers in one place.

> *Idea:*
>
> *Use colorful bins or fun boxes to keep things tidy.*

- **Make it comfortable:** Ask your parents for good lighting and a comfy chair.

> *Hint:*
>
> *A good lamp will help you read and write better.*

Set a Study Routine

See your study routine as planning for an adventure. Of course, a plan lets you know what to do and when. This is how to set up your study routine:

- **Choose a study time:** Find a time each day to study.

> *Idea:*
>
> *You can choose the time to be before dinner or right after school. Make sure you do it at the same time every day.*

- **Break it up:** Do not go for longer sessions. Break it into smaller sessions.

> *Idea:*
>
> *Study for 15–30 minutes, then take a 5-minute break. During the break, stretch, play a game, or have a snack to keep your brain fresh.*

- **Set goals:** Before studying, ask yourself, "What do I want to get done?"

> **Hint:**
>
> *Want to finish your homework or learn a new thing? With a goal, you will stay focused until you get it done.*

Stay Focused

Detectives stay focused on what they are searching for, right? That's what you should do when you study too. This is what will help you:

- **Use a timer:** Set a timer. Yes, know how long you want to study, but let the timer work in the background. Once it rings, take a break.

> **Idea:**
>
> *Use your parent's device to set a timer if there is no clock at home.*

- **Ask for help:** Ask a friend, teacher, or parent for help. They can give you tips.

With these study skills, you are all set!

Finding Answers: Research Skills and Information Gathering

Sometimes, studying can lead to "research." Research is when you have a tricky homework question or something you don't know, so you ask people or look up information to find the answer. Got it? Let's learn how to gather information the right way!

Using the Library

The library has lots of books and information. But how would you find what you need?

- **Ask the librarian:** Librarians are friendly guides. They know where everything is. So, ask them for help.

- **Look for books:** Libraries have all types of books on many topics. Look for books about the subject you are searching for.

- **Check the index:** Go to the index at the back when you find the book. It is a map that helps you find specific information in a book. Check the words related to the index topic to get to the right pages.

Searching Online

The internet is bigger than any library in the world. It has plenty of information, and you can access it from home. This is how to be smart when searching online:

- **Use safe websites:** Use websites people trust. Sites ending with ".gov" (for government) or ".edu" (for education) are often trustworthy.

- **Use the right words:** When you search online, be specific. Instead of just typing "puzzles," try "math puzzles for kids." This helps you find the correct information.

- **Check several places:** Don't use just one website. Check a few different sites for correct information.

Evaluating Information

Not all information is right, so you need to know what's true. You can do that when you

- **Check the author:** Who wrote the information? Are they experts like scientists or teachers? If so, they will provide accurate details.

> **Hint:**
>
> *If you're not sure, confirm with other authors.*

- **Look for recent information**: The information should be up-to-date. Things do change, so make sure they have the latest facts.

  - ○ ***Read carefully:*** *Make sure you understand it. If it sounds strange, check other sources.*

With this, you will be ready to get answers to any questions like a pro! So, happy searching, smart buddy!

Being a Team Player: Working Together in School Projects

Think back to the last time your teacher asked you to join a school project with others. How did it go? Was there something you felt you could do better? In this section, you will learn how to improve and be a better team player!

Teamwork

In a soccer team, some guard the goal, some kick the ball, and others cheer on their teammates. Even though they have different tasks, did you notice that they work together to reach a common goal? That is teamwork! When everyone works together for a common goal, that is teamwork.

Why Is Teamwork Important?

When building a big puzzle with friends or others, each person has a piece; when everyone puts their piece in, the puzzle will be completed. That sweet! Here are more reasons:

- **Sharing ideas:** We cannot all have the same ideas. When you work as a team, you mix ideas for better results.

- **Helping each other:** If one person is stuck, another person can help.

- **Learning from others:** You can learn new things when you work with different people.

> **Hint:**
> *If a classmate is good at drawing, another team member can learn to draw better from them.*

How You Can Become a Good Team Player

The steps to be a good team player are:

- **Listen to everyone:** Listen when others are speaking. This is because everyone's ideas are important!

- **Share your ideas:** If you have an idea, share it. Do not be shy. It might be the idea the group needs.

- **Be positive:** Encourage your team by saying, "That's a good idea!" "Good job!" or "Fantastic!" A kind word and a smile will make everyone feel better.

- **Do your part:** If everyone does their role, the project will be successful in the end.

- **Ask for help:** Not sure about something? Ask your teammates!

Fun Exercise: Teamwork Challenge

Try a teamwork exercise where you find a partner, build something or draw together, share ideas, help each other, and celebrate together.

With this, you can be a good team player!

Exam Experts: Tips for Taking Tests Without Stress

Do you find tests scary? Do not worry! I'll share some tips to help you prepare for the test with little stress.

Start Early

It is wrong to wait until the last minute before you study. So, start studying 4–5 days before the test. Do these:

- **Make a study plan:** Decide what part you will read each day.

> *Hint:*
>
> *"On Monday, I'll review math. On Tuesday, I'll review science."*

- **Break it up:** Do short study sessions. They are fun and easy!

Use Fun Study Methods

It doesn't have to be boring! Here are some fun ways to study:

- **Flash cards:** Quiz yourself and provide answers to those questions.

> **Hint:**
>
> *Ask a friend or family member to help set some questions.*

- **Songs and rhymes:** Turn important facts into a rhyme or song. Singing will help you remember!

- **Drawing:** Make colorful drawings. This will help you understand and remember information.

Get Organized

Here are some tips:

- **Gather supplies:** Keep your notes, books, pencils, and other materials needed close by.

- **Create a study space:** Use the quiet spot you have already created.

Practice Relaxation

Even if you have prepared well, you can still be worried. But these are what you can do to stay calm:

- **Take deep breaths:** Before starting your test, take a few deep breaths to help you relax.

- **Stretch:** Stretch your legs and arms to feel more comfortable.

Respect School Rules

Your schools have rules for tests. This is what you can do:

- **Read instructions carefully:** Understand what you should do before the test.

- **Ask for help:** Not sure about something? Ask your teacher!

- **Manage your time:** Note how much time you have for each question. When the time is up for one, go to the other.

Be Positive

You have prepared and done your best, so be confident that your test will be fine! You need this feeling before and even after the test.

If you apply these tips, you will take the test without stress. Yes, you've got this!

We have just summarized all the basic things you need to know about successfully learning. If you live by these rules, you will continue to be the super smart kid loved at home and school.

I have something new to share with you. Let me ask you: Would you want to learn how to earn, save, and spend money? Let's find out in the next chapter!

Chapter 13: Junior Economists— Basics of Financial Literacy

Do you have a piggy bank? Has your mom ever told you to put your spare change in it? That's a fantastic way to start saving money! But did you know that saving is just one part of learning how to handle money? You also need to learn how to earn and spend it smartly.

Think you're too young? Not at all! You're shaping the future, so learning good money habits now is cool. In this chapter, you'll discover how to earn, save, and spend money wisely. Get ready for some fun!

Money Basics: Learning About Dollars and Cents

How much do you know about dollars and cents? Maybe a little? Well, let's start with learning about dollars and cents!

What Is Money?

Imagine you have a special card that lets you get candy or toys. Money represents that special card; it helps you get things you need or want.

Different Forms of Money

Money comes in different sizes and shapes. Check out these cool ones:

- **Coins:** They are the small, shiny circles we can feel in our pockets. Coins can be nickels, pennies, dimes, and quarters. Each of them has a different value. For instance, a penny is worth one cent.

- **Bills:** These are flat pieces of paper, and sometimes they can be plastic with cool designs and numbers, like credit or debit cards. We have $100, $50, $20, $10, $5, and even $1 bills! Each of these bills differs.

For example, a $5 bill is worth five times more than a $1 bill.

Understanding the Value of Money

So, why is money important? It helps us trade what we have for what we want. Imagine that your mom has a coffee stand. She sells coffee for $1 a cup. When buyers give her $1, they trade it for her coffee. Then, she can use the $1 to buy what she needs or wants.

Making Money: First Steps to Earn It

Let us get you your first step to making money. It will be fun! Let's ride.

Your Allowance

An allowance is some money given to you by your parents regularly. It could be daily, weekly, or monthly. An allowance is one of the simplest ways to start earning money. It's like a reward for being a good kid.

Do Small House Chores

You can also earn money by doing some small jobs around the home. They can be extra things that are different from your daily house chores. Here are some ideas:

- **Dog walking:** Do you have a family dog? Offer to help take the dog for a walk.

- **Watering plants:** Help water the houseplants or the garden.

- **Organizing the playroom:** You can help in organizing the playroom.

> **Cool tip:**
>
> *If you are unsure where to start, ask your parents if there are other tasks they want you to help with.*

Start a Mini Business

You can use your creativity to make money. I have gotten you some ideas:

- **Crafts and art:** Do you love making crafts or drawing? Then, create artwork or cool handmade items you sell to friends or family. You can also consider selling old toys at a garage sale or setting up a lemonade stand.

- **Pet sitting:** If your neighbor has a pet, can you offer to take care of their pet if they are away? You could also offer to wash cars in your neighborhood.

> **Hint:**
>
> *Talk to your parents or siblings about your business idea. They can help you plan and achieve your goals and develop other great ideas.*

Save and Spend Wisely

When you start to earn money, it is important to start saving and spending it wisely. Here are some tips:

- **Save some:** Put some of that money into a savings jar or a piggy bank.

- **Spend smart:** Think well before buying something. Sometimes, it's best to save up for what you want instead of spending money immediately.

A Fun Task

Design a savings chart by drawing a big circle. Divide it into four sections. Each section represents a week. Color in a section any week you save money. It's an excellent way to see how your savings are growing!

Go ahead and try these ideas; you will love the results!

Smart Saving: How to Save for What You Want

Let's talk more about smart savings.

Why Save Money?

Have you seen a cool toy you wanted, but your parents have told that you it costs a lot of money? If you saved up your money, would you be able to get that toy without having to ask for more money? It's possible. This illustration shows that saving money is important if we want to reach our dreams, and it also teaches us how to be smart with our money!

Cool fact: *The more you save, the more money you will have.*

Setting Savings Goals

A savings goal is the savings you make because you want to buy or do something, and you plan the amount you will need to save for it. Here's the best way to set a savings goal:

- **Pick what you want:** It might be a fun game, a new toy, or even a special outing. Be sure it's something you like.

- **Decide the amount you need:** Check the price of the item or what the activity will cost. The price will now become your savings goal.

- **Set a savings plan:** Decide the amount you want to save each month or week. For instance, if you want to save $10, you can save $2 weekly. That means you need five weeks to reach your goal.

Immediate Wants vs. Long-Term Benefits

Sometimes, you might want something now, like a small toy. But if you spend your money on them, you cannot save up for big goals. So, you might need to wait to get what you want first.

- ***Think before you spend:*** *Ask yourself, "Do I want to wait longer to get something better?"*

So, start saving, and set the goal!

Wise Spending: Making Informed Choices

You wouldn't want to save all your money without ever spending anything, would you? Of course not! Saving is great. Yet, spending is great, too. So, it's important to learn how to spend money wisely! Let's learn further!

Making a Simple Budget

Think of a budget as a plan for your money. A budget assists you in spending and saving. You can create a simple budget this way:

- **List your money:** First, you must know how much you have. The money could be from gifts, allowances, birthday money, or any other means of getting money.

- **Decide what you want:** Think about your wants. Do you want a fun game, a new toy, or something else?

- **Plan your spending:** Write down how much you want to spend on an item.

Yes, that is your budget.

For example, if you make $10 every month, you might set a budget that only requires you to spend $6–$7. What will happen to the leftovers? Save them!

Needs vs. Wants

Do you know the difference between needs and wants? Let's find out:

- **Needs:** They are things you need. These are clothes, food, or school items. These are important for daily living.

- **Wants:** You'd love to get them, but you don't need them immediately. For example, a new game is cool and fun, but it is not necessary.

Task

When you next want to buy something, confirm if it is a need or a want. Do that every time to spend money wisely.

Money Management: Planning and Tracking

It's time to learn how you can handle money like a pro. Let's enjoy the tips together!

What Is Money Management?

Well, money management might seem like a big word, but it is simply about planning and tracking your money. Adults use money management to save for big things, to pay bills, and to buy things!

Tracking Your Money

Now is the time to track where your money goes. The idea is to know whether you obey your budget or not. Here's how to do it:

- **Write down where you spend your money:** Keep a small note to write down every time you spend money. Take note of the amount it costs.

- **Check your savings:** Find out regularly how much you have saved. Compare that amount to your plan to see if you're on track.

- **Adjust if you need to:** If you spend more than you planned, don't worry. Adjust your plan next time so you can spend less or save more.

Cool Exercise

Create a simple chart with columns for:

- *Date*

- *What You Bought*

- *Amount Spent*

Each time you spend money, fill in the chart.

> **Hint:**
> *Use colorful stickers or markers to make it fun!*

The Value of Spending Wisely

Wise spending is all about making smart decisions about how to spend money. Here's how to be wise:

- **Think before buying:** Before buying anything, think about it. Ask if it's something you want and if it fits into all you have calculated to be your budget.

- **Compare prices:** If you want to buy something, look at different places for the best price.

- **Save for special things**: If you want something big, save up for it. When you save, you will be able to get what you want.

Fun Challenge

Ask anyone who wants to buy something if they have checked the best deals.

Why Is Money Management Important?

It will help you buy the things you want without running out of money. It also teaches you how to be responsible with your money, making you the captain of your money.

With this, you can manage your money like a pro!

You've just learned some cool tips on how to make and manage money! Now, it's time to apply those tips and become the captain of your money. Ready to sail? Wish you safe travels!

In the next chapter, you will learn about the world of games and hobbies. I'll be waiting for you.

Chapter 14: Entertainment Wizards—Exploring Games and Hobbies

Games and hobbies are super important, no matter how old you are! When you hear the sound of your favorite game, you probably can't wait to jump in and play. Guess what? You're not alone!

This chapter will explore the fun world of games and hobbies. You will discover why they're so important and how to balance playing structured games, like soccer or chess, with unstructured play, like drawing or building with blocks. We'll also look at exciting outdoor activities and cozy indoor games.

So, find your favorite spot and get ready to explore all the cool things you can do for fun. Let's go!

Why Playing Is Important: Learning Through Fun

Playing might seem fun and exciting, but it's much more than that! It helps you learn new things and grow. In this section, you will learn why playing is so amazing and how it will help you become even more awesome!

The Importance of Play

Each time you play, you do something more than enjoy a good time. Playing helps us improve many skills and learn new things. Imagine building a big castle with blocks. Of course, you are having fun stacking blocks, but did you know that the play is teaching you about sizes, shapes, and how you can balance things? Isn't that cool? Yes!

You Learn Through Play

Playing helps the brain grow. When playing an indoor or outdoor game, your brain will work well to know how to win or solve a problem. An example is when you are playing a puzzle game. A puzzle game uses your brain to think about where to put each piece. Regularly playing this game will improve your problem-solving skills and help you think smart.

Different Types of Play

We have just two types of play. They are

- **Structured play:** Structured play has rules and plans. Examples are following a recipe for cooking or playing a board game. Structured play is nice because it helps you learn to follow rules and work with others.

- **Unstructured play:** Unstructured play has no set rules. Examples are making up a game or running around in the park. This type of play is important because it will help open your creativity and imagination. Unstructured play teaches you that you can be anything you put your heart to.

Finding the Balance

Did you notice that both structured and unstructured play have benefits? Yes! What does this mean? You must balance and have both types of play in your day. Structured play helps players learn to 'follow rules,' while unstructured play helps them relax and open their creativity. These types of play are great for a healthy and happy life.

So, playing isn't just fun. You need it to grow and learn!

Playing Outside: Fun Outdoor Activities

Playing outside allows you to move around, check new things, and breathe fresh air. It's a great way to keep your mind happy and your body strong. There are lots of cool outdoor activities that are fun and good for you. Let's walk you through some of these awesome outdoor activities and learn why they are good for your body and mind!

Sports and Games

Sports is a great way to have fun outside. Playing basketball, soccer, or even tag with your friends when you play outside is possible. Sports can help you get active, stay healthy, and build muscle. Plus, they can teach good skills like teamwork. Imagine when you run around with your friends and laugh together.

Nature Walks and Exploring

Have you ever taken a nature walk? These outdoor activities help you discover amazing things in nature. You can see cute animals, colorful flowers, or even beautiful rocks. Nature walks are great. They help people relax and learn about the world that surrounds them. It's like having a nice adventure each time you are outside.

Outdoor Adventures

These can be playing in the park or hiking on a trail. You can swing high on swings, climb jungle gyms, or build sandcastles at the beach. While fun, these activities will help you stay healthy and fit. Plus, they will help you get creative and improve your imagination.

Benefits for Your Body and Mind

When you jump, run, and play, your heart stays healthy and your body becomes strong.

Playing outside also helps your mind. When you are in nature, you can feel calm and happy. It's an excellent way to be free from screens and enjoy fresh air.

How to Have Fun Outside

Explore these easy ideas to get started:

- **Play a sport:** Get a ball and play with friends or family.

- **Go on a nature walk:** Walk your backyard or a beautiful park and check what you can see and find.

- **Have an outdoor picnic:** Go outside with your favorite snacks and enjoy it in the fresh air.

- **Build something:** Use leaves, sticks, or sand to create your outdoor masterpiece.

Get outside to start your next adventure today!

Fun Inside: Board Games, Stories, and Arts

Just like outdoor games, there are tons of exciting games you can play inside! This section will explore some awesome indoor activities to help your brain grow!

Board Games with Friends and Family

Games like Scrabble, Monopoly, Chess, or Ludo can make players think and laugh. Each time you play board games, you use your brain to follow rules and make decisions. It also offers a great way to spend time with friends and family.

Ideas

- Scrabble
- Monopoly
- Chess
- Ludo
- Whot
- Card games
- Scavenger hunt
- Hide and seek

Reading Stories: Adventures in Books

Books can take you on fantastic adventures while you are in the comfort of your house. Reading lets you learn about our world, meet pleasant characters, and enjoy fun journeys. Whether it's a funny story, a mystery, or a thriller, books will help you learn new things and expand your imagination.

> *Hint:*
>
> *Find a cozy spot in your home, grab a book, and have fun traveling. You can also read with friends and family members for more fun!*

Arts and Crafts

You can paint, draw, or build. Make a colorful picture with crayons or use clay to build something. Arts and crafts are fun and will help you get better at using your hands. It will also help you think creatively. And finally, you can show off the amazing things you have created to your family!

Imaginative Play

This type of play involves using your imagination to create fun play, adventures, and stories. It might involve pretending to be a superhero saving something or a chef cooking something in an imaginary kitchen. Imaginative play helps you think creatively and solve problems in special ways.

> *Idea:*
>
> *Use your imagination to start the coolest adventures.*

The Role of Indoor Games

Board games help with problem-solving and thinking. Reading improves your imagination and language skills; arts and crafts boost fine motor and creativity skills.

Next time you're inside, try and do one of these awesome things!

Family Game Night: Enjoying Time with Family

Family game night is a special time to be together with your family, have fun, and create happy memories. It is just how it sounds—a night for everyone to play games in the family. So, let's get some ideas here.

Fun Games for Family Game Night

- **Board games:** Ideas include family favorites like Candy Land, Monopoly, and Scrabble. Everyone can sit around the table to enjoy the game.

- **Card games:** These are cool because one can play them with a deck of cards. Ideas include Uno, Go Fish, or Crazy Eights. They are simple to learn and perfect for all in the family.

- **Charades:** This game involves acting out phrases or words without saying a word. Family members must guess what the person is acting out.

- **Pictionary:** This involves drawing a picture of something, and the other players will guess what it is.

- **Puzzle games:** All family members will work together to solve a puzzle. It helps the family bond while they are putting the pieces together.

Making Game Night Special

- **Pick only favorite games:** Let everyone choose their favorite game. Then, you can take turns picking the games each week.

- **Create a cozy space:** Get blankets and snacks like cookies and popcorn.

- **Make it a tradition:** Make family game night a regular event. It could be every weekend or any other time that works for your family.

- **Celebrate wins and laughs:** The most important part is the fun. It is not about who won or who lost.

So, if you do not win for a night, enjoy the game with others!

Why Family Game Night Is Awesome

Family game night is a great way to help everyone stay closer. Playing games together makes you talk, laugh, and work as a team. So, be there to share joy and create amazing memories!

> *Idea:*
>
> *When the family has a free evening, suggest a family game night to Mom and Dad. It is a fun way to show you care about your family.*

Ready to roll the dice and have some fun? Game on!

I am sure you are now ready to explore the world of games and hobbies fully—indoors, outdoors, and during family nights!

Yes, adventure is fun! But what are the basics of survival and exploring nature? Let's find out in the next chapter!

Chapter 15: Adventurers—Basics of Survival and Exploring Nature

Do you find nature interesting? Do you enjoy looking closely at tiny things, especially those near the ground? If you do, you're going to love exploring nature! This chapter will give you all the information you need to start your adventure. Are you set? Let's go!

Getting Ready for Camping: Packing and Planning

Before heading out camping, you have to do many cool things to get ready. Let's now dive into how to prepare for the camping trip.

Packing Smart

Here's what you'll need:

- **Tent:** A tent is a cozy home away from home. Therefore, it must be big enough for the number of people going. Also, go with the stakes to keep it in shape.

- **Sleeping bag:** You need a sleeping bag to stay warm at night. When Mom and Dad pick one, remind them to pick one appropriate for the weather.

- **Clothes:** Wear clothes perfect for camping—warm clothes for chilly evenings, cool ones for sunny or hot days, and a rain jacket just in case.

- **Food and water:** Pack fruits and snacks like granola bars. You can also pack easy-to-cook food. Always carry plenty of water.

- **First aid kit:** The kit or box must have antiseptic, band-aids, and anything to fix small scrapes or cuts.

Outdoor Navigation Basics

If you are ready, let's learn how to find your way in the wild!

- **Using a compass:** A compass will help you know where you're going. The compass comes with a needle. This needle always points north. When using it, stand still and hold the compass flat. Rotate your body until the needle points to "N" on the compass. When that happens, that is the direction you're facing!

- **Reading a map:** Maps show the locations of rivers, trails, and campsites. Look for places like mountains or trees. Maps come with a "key" that explains the meaning of symbols.

Why Preparation Is Key

If you go with the right gear and have learned how to find your way, you will have safer and funner adventures! It is important to be with Mom and Dad when they are preparing.

> *Task:*
>
> *When the family is going camping next, offer to keep a checklist of all that the family needs and tick the boxes to confirm that you are all set!*

So, it is now time to pack and enjoy nature!

Nature's Rules: Tips for Wilderness Survival

Nature can be super fun. However, learning how to stay safe and enjoy the adventure is important. Let's enjoy some great tips you need!

Building a Shelter

If you want camping, you need a shelter to stay cozy and dry. Here's how to build one:

- **Use a good spot:** A flat area free from where water might collect is fine. Do not use near streams or under big trees.

- **Use nature's tools:** Join others in gathering branches, leaves, and sticks. Be there as they arrange the sticks to form a teepee shape. Then, they should use branches and leaves to cover it.

- **Check your shelter:** Remind an adult to check for gaps where rain can get in. The shelter must be comfy!

Finding Water and Food

What if you run out of water and fruit? Let's find out:

- **Finding water:** Look for rivers, streams, or a damp area for water. Not sure it is safe? Boil the water or use a water filter to make it safe for drinking.

- **Finding food:** You might find fruit or nuts in the forest. Of course, be sure they are safe. You can also catch small animals or fish. If you cannot do any of that, know how to ration the packaged food in your backpack well.

Basics of First Aid

An accident can happen at any time, so if it happens, practice everything you learned in Chapter 10 about emergencies and accidents!

Safe Fire-Making

You need fire to cook and stay warm. To start the fire, collect sticks and dry leaves. Next, dig a small hole and circle it with rocks. Finally, light it with lighters or matches. Never leave it unattended.

What to Do When Lost

Sometimes, you can get a little lost. Do these when that happens:

- **Be calm:** Don't panic so you can think clearly.

- **Find a landmark:** Find something to help you remember where you are. It can be a rock, a tree, or a river.

- **Use the compass and map:** Check your compass and map. If you're not sure, remain where you are to wait for help.

- **Call for help:** Yell loudly. If you have a radio or phone, use it.

With these, you are all set for any adventure in nature!

Discovering Nature: Learning About Plants and Animals

Let us learn the categories of plants and animals that are safe and dangerous.

Meet the Plants

Plants keep our air clean and offer food to animals. This is how to get to know them:

- **Wildflowers:** Search for colorful wildflowers in forests and meadows. They can be blue, red, yellow, or purple! Although fun, not all of them are safe to eat or touch.

- **Trees:** They are the giant guys in the forest. Each tree has its special flowers, leaves, and sometimes, fruits. For example, you might find pines, oaks, and maples in the forest. What sets the trees apart is their leaves—small and needle-like or big and broad.

- **Bushes and shrubs:** Bushes and shrubs are smaller than trees. In some bushes, there are berries for animals to eat. Before you eat or touch any berries, ask an adult.

Note: *Before going into the wild, find out what dangerous plants and animals are there and how to behave when you see one. Also, learn first aid treatment to apply if you come into contact with any of them.*

Watch Out for the Wild Side

Plants to avoid:

- **Poison ivy:** Touching it can cause itchy rashes. It has just three shiny leaves. Don't touch it or go close to it.

- **Thorny bushes:** There are some bushes with sharp thorns. If you get close, they will scratch you.

Spotting Animals

Let us now talk about animals that stay in the wild!

- **Birds:** There are different types of birds in the wild. You will find eagles, owls, robins, and more when you look up. The birds sing songs, and each bird comes with a different tune.

- **Insects:** Small insects like bees, ladybugs, or butterflies keep flowers growing and help spread pollen. Watch them playing around.

- **Mammals:** Animals like rabbits, squirrels, and deer can be seen in parks and forests. Some are quick, while some are shy.

Staying Safe and Respectful

When venturing into nature, it's essential to prioritize safety and show respect for the environment around you. Below are some tips to stay safe and respectful:

- **Don't touch everything:** Some animals could scratch or bite you. Remember, some plants can be itchy. Ask an adult if you're not sure about something.

- **Leave no trace:** If you spot something cool, that's awesome! But do not take it; let other explorers find it, too. Just observe and leave!

- **Observe, don't disturb:** Watch from a distance; do not catch them.

Yes, you are all set to explore the wild!

As you explore nature and the outdoors, how can you help care for the environment and be an awesome friend to nature? We'll find out in the next chapter!

Chapter 16: Guardians of the Planet—Environmental Responsibility

Imagine you're in charge of caring for our planet earth! How would you do it? Don't worry if you're unsure yet—I'll show you how to help our world stay happy and healthy in this chapter.

You'll learn about how everything in nature is connected, understand climate change, and learn fun ways to make a difference. Get ready to be an earth-saving hero!

Nature's Network: How Everything Connects

Let's start with learning how everything in nature connects.

What Is Ecology?

Ecology is a word that explains the study of how animals, plants, and even small bugs live and work together in nature.

The trees give oxygen that humans and animals use to breathe. Humans and animals give out carbon dioxide, and that is what the trees and plants depend on to live. To keep forests healthy, some animals and tiny bugs live in the trees and help break down leaves into soil. All of these work together to make sure the forest is healthy.

This relationship I just explained is called an *ecosystem*. An ecosystem is the interaction and cooperation of all living things and their environment.

What Is Biodiversity?

Another big word to learn is *biodiversity*. It simply means having all types of living things, like animals, plants, and insects, present.

Biodiversity is necessary because if one living thing is missing, it can mess up the ecosystem.

Do you now see why we should keep our environment full of life? It's like a sports team that needs all its players to win.

The Weather Around Us

The weather now seems different from many years back. Do you know why? It is because of *climate change.* You see, climate change is like when our earth is getting a large, warm blanket it doesn't need. So, you are thinking: What caused it? I'll tell you!

Our earth has a way of staying cool and warm. But when we burn things like gas or coal, lots of gases are sent into the air. These gases trap the heat from the sun, making the earth warmer than it should be, which will change the weather.

How You Can Help

Imagine that you decided you would eat all your cookies at once. You want to eat it little by little so it lasts long. It is the same with the earth. We all have to use the resources wisely and care for them so they can last.

There are lots of things you can do to care for the environment. Here are some ways:

- **Recycling waste:** Throw any used items that say "recycle" on them into a recycle bin.

- **Planting and caring for trees:** Join Mom and Dad in your garden. This helps provide oxygen and saves water.

- **Small actions:** Turn off lights when not needed, pick up litter, and do not throw litter around.

Eco Warriors: Ways to Conserve Nature and Energy

We should talk more about how you can care for nature and use the earth's resources well.

Recycling: The Magic of Reusing

It is not only big companies that can recycle. You, too, can recycle! When you recycle, you turn things like cans, bottles, and paper into new items instead of throwing them in the trash.

A Task for You

- Ask your parents to set up a recycle bin at home. (You can even make a DIY recycle box.)

- Weekly, sort the items in there and keep the ones you can recycle. (For example, an empty plastic bottle can serve as a sprinkler, planter, paint or pen holder, and many more. Check how you can do that online.)

Note: *That's for plastic bottles alone. You can search for DIY ways to use other items.*

Composting: Nature's Super Snack

So, what is composting? It is like making a different soil type from leftover vegetables or food. Use this task to know how it works.

A Task for You

- Put vegetable scraps, fruit peels, coffee grounds, leaves, and eggshells into a different bin.

- Mix them and wait! (Worms and bugs will eat them.)

- After some months, this compost will become rich dark soil. It is good for your plants to grow.

Warning: Keep it far away from the house. Do not add meat, oily food, or plastic. Stir once in a while to allow air in. Add a little water. Be patient!

Saving Water: Every Drop Counts

We all know that water is precious. Therefore, you must use it wisely.

A Task for You

- Watch an adult fix leaks and do the same under the adult's supervision.

- Every day, do something that saves water.

Saving Energy: Bright Ideas

When you use less energy, you can help the planet.

A Task for You

- Make it a daily goal to always turn off lights and other electronics when not in use. Encourage your parents to use only energy-efficient light bulbs.

- Always unplug chargers and devices when no one is using them.

The Eco Warrior Task

- In your family, create what you will call a "Green Action Plan."

- List all the ways you can compost, recycle, save energy, and save water.

- Each one should choose one action and then track progress.

- Make a colorful poster that will remind everyone of the family's goal.

With these, you will join the people who keep our earth happy and clean. Every little action you take will make a big difference.

So, start saving the planet today!

I'm glad to call you a good citizen of the earth. But do you know that people in society need you, too? In the next chapter, you will learn how to contribute to society and the world!

Chapter 17: Little Citizens— Contributing to Society and the World

Hey, little citizen! You are one of the leaders of tomorrow! Do you know what that means for you? That means you have a special job: making the world a better place. Now is the best time to start helping the society and the world. Do you know why? The sooner you start, the more awesome things you can do—for yourself and everyone around you.

In this chapter, we will explore your role, learn some cool new words, and understand the power you have now to make a difference in the world. Sounds exciting, right? Let's start the journey now!

Rights and Rules: What They Mean for Us

Did you know we all have important rights and special rules? Let us now talk about what they mean and their importance.

What Are Rights?

Rights are the things you are able to enjoy because you are you! Check out these few examples:

- **Freedom of speech:** This means you have the right to think and express your own ideas. Each time you think and share ideas, you are using that right.

- **Right to education:** This right means that you can learn at school and add something new to your brain.

- **Right to play:** It means having fun and enjoying games with friends. When you play, you grow happy and strong.

What Are Responsibilities?

It's time to talk about *responsibilities*. Responsibilities will help you to use your right well. You see, responsibilities are like rules for caring for things and making sure everything works well. Below are some examples:

- **Respect the rules:** There are rules in the community where you live that help everyone stay connected and close. Following these rules helps keep things safe and fair.

- **Respect others:** It's good to be kind and respectful. This ensures that everyone feels comfortable and happy.

- **Help out:** Helping others is part of your responsibilities. Can you share your toys or lend a hand?

Why Are They Important?

Your rights and responsibilities are good friends. They work together. We need them to make this world a nice place to live. These are ways our rights help us:

- **Building trust:** Each time you follow rules, people will trust you. Trust is like a bridge that connects people.

- **Creating fairness:** When you respect everyone's rights, it creates balance, and everyone will be able to enjoy their rights.

- **Being a team player:** Working together and respecting the rules helps everybody enjoy a good time and reach their goal!

So, you see that you have a role: Know your rights and use them responsibly. This will make the world a good place. Is that cool? Yes, it is!

Lending a Hand: How to Help in Your Community

This section will introduce you to the practical ways you can help your community. Let's start with volunteering.

What Is Volunteering?

Volunteering is when you decide to help others without thinking of getting something from them. So, here are some cool ways to volunteer:

- **Helping at a local event:** Your town might have a festival at one point. Can you greet people, set up, or even clean up after the festival is over?

- **Assisting at animal shelters:** Do you love animals? If yes, you can help at a shelter. You can feed pets, give them attention and love, and clean their spaces.

- **Participating in cleanup days:** When there are days where people pick up trash around the neighborhood or parks in your community, join in.

Note: Your parents must allow you to do so. Ask an older adult to care for your well-being while volunteering. If your parents volunteer, join them!

Why Is Helping Important?

Helping others makes everyone in the community feel good and makes your community a cool place to live. Each time you help, you are telling others, even people you do not know, that you care.

Becoming Parts of a Local Project

Sometimes, your community might be doing a special project. These special projects need helpers. Volunteering can be exciting and fun.

For example

- **Planting gardens:** Help plant vegetables or flowers.

- **Reading to younger kids:** You can read stories to children younger than you are at school or in the library. These kids will enjoy the stories, and you'll be happy to share it with them.

- **Creating art:** Paint a mural or join in decorate for an event coming up in the community.

How Does It Feel to Help?

Do you feel happy when others smile because of you? So, when you do something that benefits the whole community, the whole community will be happy with you. Imagine all of them giving you a warm hug.

You can also learn new things as you help, meet good people who have volunteered, and guess what? You can make long-lasting friends!

Changing the World: Understanding Global Challenges

Our world faces a lot of big challenges. You can be one of those who will solve them. We will call this problem a "global challenge." So, let's get to work!

What Are Global Challenges?

We can define global challenges as big problems facing everyone in the world. Here are a few of these challenges:

- **Climate change:** This happens when our beautiful earth becomes warmer because of smoke from factories, cars, and other things.

- **Inequality:** Access to resources and opportunities varies significantly among individuals. For example, some people might not get enough water, education, or food, while others have them in surplus.

- **Sustainable development:** This is about using resources without harming the planet. This will allow future children to enjoy the world.

How Can You Help?

These problems are big. But there are things you can do to help. Let's check out some of them:

- **Learn and share:** Read about climate challenges through books, school projects, or documentaries.

Share it with your classmates, family, and friends when you learn something new. Remember, the more people know, the more help they will offer.

- **Support fairness:** Be fair and kind to everyone. If someone is not treated well, speak up. Do not remain silent. However, be respectful when you speak.

- **Get involved:** Join community or school projects that address saving energy, water, and recycling. The community might need you to clean up, plant trees, or support local charities.

Why Is It Important to Help?

When you help with global challenges, you make the world a better place. Any attempt to save the earth's resources will make a positive difference. Small actions will lead to big changes! If you share the things you learn with others, will move them to join in, too. Think of it as a chain.

So, helping with global challenges will create a reaction of care and kindness. Are you ready to start making big changes? Welcome!

If you apply all these tips, you will be a good citizen of the world, and one day, your name will be known all over the world.

Great trip so far, not so? Yeah! It's time for the final life skill to learn. In the next chapter, you will learn how to keep learning forever!

Chapter 18: Growth Stars—Your Path to Continuous Self-Improvement

You might be thinking, "Yay! I've read a lot, and now I can relax!" Well, that's okay. After working hard, it's great to take a break. But guess what? When it comes to learning, the fun never stops! Learning is something you will keep doing forever.

In this chapter, we talk about why it's great to keep learning forever. I will show you how to be open to new things, set goals for yourself, and try new things. You'll see how to use the skills you've learned in this book to solve new problems and continue growing. The chapter will help you to be ready to learn and excited about what's next!

Never Stop Learning: How New Discoveries Make Us Stronger

We'll now talk about the reason why you should not stop learning. Let us start with what lifelong learning is supposed to be.

What Is Lifelong Learning?

The term "lifelong learning" means you will always keep learning new things as you grow. There will be no end. After school or after learning something new, learning will still not stop. You will keep learning and trying different and new things daily.

Why Is Learning Important?

Learning will help you:

- **Solve small and big problems:** Every time you learn new things, you will be better at solving problems. For instance, if you learn to fix a bike, you will ride better and be able to help others with their bikes.

- **Adapt to change:** The world keeps changing. There are new things made, new styles of doing things, and even new ideas. When you keep learning, you will be able to follow up with these changes and be ready for anything.

- **Explore interests:** Do you love drawing? Learning a new style can improve your drawings and make you want to try new things you have never done before.

How Do You Keep Learning?

Let's check some ways to make learning a big part of your life:

- **Read books:** Did you learn a lot from this book? I know you would. Now, just imagine how many lessons you will learn from other books!

> *Idea:*
> *Read books on any topic. You can start from adventures, plants, or animals.*

- **Ask questions:** If you don't know how something works, just ask. You may be surprised at how much you will learn.

- **Try new things:** Sometimes, it is not bad to try something new like a hobby or sport. You will not be good at first, but keep learning to get better.

- **Watch educational shows:** You can watch lots of fun videos and shows that teach you fine skills and facts. Do not forget to watch them with a grown-up who will help you know what you are watching.

Yes! Do not stop learning! It will help you adapt and grow! Are you ready to welcome the adventure of learning? Good for you!

Bend, Don't Break: How to Adapt and Succeed

On your way to success, you will come across many problems. They will want to break you. But don't break, only bend. Let's see how you can do that here!

What Is Adaptability and Flexibility?

The word "adaptability" defines your ability to handle changes and still do well. Flexibility is your ability to change when things don't go as you expect. Just imagine a tree, bracing itself against the wind. The tree bends but does not break. Be that tree if you want to succeed.

The Importance of Adaptability and Flexibility

Adaptability and flexibility are important traits that help people deal with life's uncertainties and challenges. Here are some reasons why adaptability and flexibility matter:

- **It helps you handle change:** Sometimes, a good plan can fail. For example, Mom can change your bedtime. If you are flexible, you will be able to accept and adjust to that change.

- **It helps you face challenges:** You won't like tough homework. But by being adaptable, you will be able to find many ways to solve it. If one way does not work, the other will.

- **It helps you make new friends:** You might meet a new person who loves something different. But if you are adaptable, you will be able to find what you both like or even learn what they love.

How to Be Flexible and Adaptable

These easy tips will help:

- **Always welcome new ideas:** When a friend or family member suggests a new way of doing

The Ultimate Kids' Guide to Life Skill

something, check it out! In this book, you might have read things you have never heard before. Try them out. You will see something fun that you didn't expect.

- **Always think:** If your plan for something fails, think of another way. Do not just stop. For example, if it rains and you cannot play outside, use the indoor suggestions in this book.

- **Be positive:** Again, if what you wanted to do did not work well, instead of being angry, be positive and look for more ways to get it done.

- **Learn from mistakes:** We all make mistakes. When you make mistakes, do not be too sad. Learn from those mistakes. Just think about how you can do that thing differently next time.

So, let these be your guide. You will achieve many great things!

Dreams and Goals: Planning How to Make Them Real

Do you sometimes dream of being a famous person in the future? Maybe you want to be an astronaut, an artist, a doctor, a footballer, or an engineer. Those dreams are super cool. But let's see how you can make them real.

Your Dream Needs Goals

Dreams are not enough. To make them come true, they need plans and goals. So, the next question should be: Why are dreams and goals important?

Why Are Dreams and Goals Important?

Dreams represent the big ideas or aspirations you have for your future, while goals are the actionable steps you will take to turn those dreams into reality. For example, you might dream of becoming an astronaut, and your goals would involve learning about space, studying science, and completing relevant training.

The Importance of Goals

- **It helps you focus:** With goals, you have something to work on. This will not let you give up.

- **It makes your dream clear:** Goals help you break dreams into small steps. When you know the next step, you will know what to do.

- **It tracks your steps:** You will see what you have done when you set goals. Knowing this will help you get closer to your dream.

How to Set Goals

Here are the steps you can take to set goals:

- **Start with your dream:** Think about your big dream. Write them down. You can even draw a picture of it.

- **Set clear goals:** Break the big dream into smaller goals. For example, if you want to be a famous footballer, have a goal to practice every week.

- **Make a plan:** You will tell yourself what to do to hit your goal. For example, a plan could be to practice football for two hours weekly.

- **Ask for help:** Sometimes, you will need help. Your friends or teachers can help with it. These people will give you advice.

- **Keep trying:** It might be hard to get to your goals. If that happens, keep trying and be positive. Do not forget that every step will take you to your dream.

Think about all the skills you have learned in this guide. Do you know that those skills will help you to achieve your dream? So, keep your dream alive and use all these skills to achieve them.

Saying "Yes" to New Adventures: Jumping into New Experiences

Every day opens an opportunity to try something new. So, let's talk about what will make you always say "yes" to new things.

Why Should You Always Try New Things?

Trying new things can be an experience that opens up a world of possibilities and personal growth. Below are a few reasons why you should try new things:

- **You will learn new skills:** New activities, like learning a new game, reading a new book, or cooking a new recipe, will give you new skills.

- **You will meet new friends:** Trying new things can help you meet new people who love the same thing.

- **You will have fun:** New things can be fun and exciting. When you try something new, you might love it very much.

- **You will grow and improve:** Each time you try a new thing, you will be able to learn more about yourself. You will also be able to learn about what you like and get better at doing different things.

How You Can Welcome New Adventures

These tips will help:

- **Be willing:** When you hear about something new like a new book or game, be willing to try it and ask questions to learn more about it.

- **Take baby steps:** Start a new thing with small steps. For example, if you want to try a new game, watch it while others play or watch it on TV.

- **Be bold:** Are you scared to try something new? That's okay! When you are bold, you will want to try it anyway. You will be surprised how much you enjoy it.

- **Enjoy the trip:** Do not always forget that the goal is to have fun as you learn, even if things do not happen the way you like. What you have done so far has taught you a lesson.

- **Share your experience:** Talk to family and friends about that new thing. Who knows, they might want to join you! When you share, the experience will become more fun!

When there is an opportunity to learn something new, you should say, "yes." If you always do that, you will learn a lot and become better every day!

Before you finally take your leave, let us talk about what you have learned so far in this book on the next page!

Conclusion: The Never-Ending Journey—Growing Up and Beyond

Wow! What an exciting adventure we've had! You know what's super cool? I'm so proud of you, and I am sure that you are well on your way to becoming a superhero! But hold on. Do you think the journey to growth and learning has ended? Not at all! This journey is just beginning. Well, how about we quickly review some of the cool things we've learned together?

Was it not cool to learn about yourself? Now, you can learn more about your strengths, feelings, and what makes you special. All of these will help you become more aware of your surroundings and help you be bold. Remember, even though we all look different, everyone is special and can improve the world. Are you ready to show respect and kindness to everyone you meet? Good decision there!

With the lessons you learned about doing things yourself, I know you are more ready to help at home and do many chores. You're not just a helper; you're making a big difference! How about those tips about handling money? Did you not find it awesome to learn how to earn, save, and spend wisely? That's going to be super useful now and in the future!

What about taking care of our environment? You enjoyed learning about recycling, saving water and energy, and keeping your surroundings clean. If you have started doing that, keep up the great work.

Was learning to keep improving yourself a great way to end this guide? Yes, it was! Just remember, learning is a never-ending adventure. Keep going and keep growing!

I hope you enjoyed the fun activities and games—we sure had a blast! Keep practicing, and remember: You're doing amazing things! *The Ultimate Kids' Guide to Life Skills* has given you awesome skills for your learning journey ahead.

So, keep exploring and keep learning. This guide is just the start of your exciting journey. Keep discovering new things, and you'll never regret it.

You're doing great, and I'm excited to see all the awesome things you'll do next!

Goodbye for now, and remember to keep shining bright!

References

Admin. (2023, November 16). *Top 10 safety rules for kids at school.* Simpli English. https://simplienglish.com/blog/top-10-safety-rules-for-kids-at-school/

Afrikindness. (2023, May). *Exploring cultural diversity: Empowering children to embrace differences and thrive.* LinkedIn. https://www.linkedin.com/pulse/exploring-cultural-diversity-empowering-children-embrace/

American Psychological Association. (2012). *Resilience guide for parents and teachers.* American Psychological Association. https://www.apa.org/topics/resilience/guide-parents-teachers

Anger, M. (n.d.). *A child therapist's favorite resources for helping kids manage anger.* Coping Skills for Kids. https://copingskillsforkids.com/managing-anger

Annon. (2022, February 25). *Self-regulation vs self-control: What's the difference?* London School of Childcare Studies. https://childcarestudies.co.uk/2022/02/25/self-regulation-vs-self-control-whats-the-difference/

Anon. (2021, February 25). *Self-care ideas for kids.* Understood. https://www.understood.org/en/articles/self-care-for-kids-6-ways-to-self-regulate

Anon. (2022, August 12). *Helping kids identify and express their feelings.* Big Heart Toys. https://bighearttoys.com/blogs/emotional-behavioral/how-does-a-child-express-their-feelings-through-behaviour

Anon. (2024). *What makes children angry.* American Psychological Association. https://www.apa.org/act/resources/fact-sheets/children-angry

Ansari, S. (2022, August 13). *How art therapy can help relieve kids from stress?* PiggyRide. https://www.piggyride.com/blog/how-art-therapy-can-help-relieve-kids-from-stress/

Art. (2019, November 18). *Friendship skills: Helping kids to master the art of being a friend.* Ann Douglas. https://www.anndouglas.net/blog/2019/11/18/helping-kids-to-master-the-art-of-being-a-friend

Ayres, N. (2024, February 10). *Embracing diversity: Art in early childhood education.* Big Hearts Little Hands. https://bighearts-littlehands.com/embracing-diversity-art-in-early-childhood-education/

Childhood depression: What parents need to know. (n.d.). Kids Health. https://kidshealth.org/en/parents/understanding-depression.html

Children's Rehabilitation Institute (2023, September 26). *Tips for staying positive in difficult times.* https://critusa.org/tips-for-staying-positive-in-difficult-times/

Connections Academy (2022, October). *How to raise smart kids: 10 secrets.* Connections Academy. https://www.connectionsacademy.com/support/resources/article/how-to-raise-smart-kids-10-secrets/

Cruze, R. (2023, October 9). *15 ways to teach kids about money.* Ramsey Solutions. https://www.ramseysolutions.com/relationships/how-to-teach-kids-about-money?

Cruze, R. (2024, April 23). *How to make money as a kid: 16 great ideas.* Ramsey Solutions.

https://www.ramseysolutions.com/saving/how-to-make-money-as-a-kid?

Cullins, A. (2017, May 17). *7 activities to help your child develop a positive attitude.* Big Life Journal. https://biglifejournal.com/blogs/blog/children-positive-attitude

Edlynn, E. (2023, August). *How can I teach my kid to stand up for himself?* Parents. https://www.parents.com/parenting/better-parenting/advice/ask-your-mom/how-can-i-teach-my-kid-to-stand-up-for-himself/

Emily. (2023, September 6). *How to recognize signs of sadness in children and show your support.* Dayton Children's Hospital. https://www.childrensdayton.org/the-hub/oosblog-how-recognize-signs-sadness-children-and-show-your-support

15 ways to engage kids in nature. (2020, June 24). Mulhall's. https://mulhalls.com/garden-home/blog/15-ways-to-engage-kids-in-nature/

Good habits for kids: Creating healthy lifestyle habits at a young age. (n.d.). Premier Education. https://www.premier-education.com/news/good-habits-for-kids-creating-healthy-lifestyle-habits-at-a-young-age/

Guest Contributor. (2024, June 28). *Teaching kids the art of friendship.* Mobile Bay Parents. https://mobilebayparents.com/2024/06/teaching-kids-the-art-of-friendship/

Gupta, S. (2023, May 26). *The importance of self-reflection.* Verywell Mind. https://www.verywellmind.com/self-reflection-importance-benefits-and-strategies-7500858

Hall, T. (2024, January 5). *Teaching children the basics of first aid and safety.* MyCPR NOW.

https://cprcertificationnow.com/blogs/mycpr-now-blog/teaching-children-the-basics-of-first-aid-and-safety

Hanigan, A. (2024, August 27). *The effects of screen time on children: The latest research parents should know.* Children's Health Hub. https://health.choc.org/the-effects-of-screen-time-on-children-the-latest-research-parents-should-know/

Harmony. (2017, June 27). *5 benefits of quality family time.* Harmony Early Education. https://harmonylearning.com.au/5-benefits-of-quality-family-time/

Helping our kids navigate our digital world. (n.d.). TELUS. https://mediasmarts.ca/sites/default/files/guides/guide_helping_kids_navigate_digital_world.pdf

HMS Administrator. (2018, January 8). *Embracing diversity from a young age.* Hollis Montessori School. https://hollismontessori.org/blog/2018/2/14/embracing-diversity-from-a-young-age

How should children balance outdoor activities and indoor ones? (n.d.). Quora. https://www.quora.com/How-should-children-balance-outdoor-activities-and-indoor-ones

Jode. (2020, February 17). *How can educators make self reflection fun for young children.* The Empowered Educator. https://www.theempowerededucatoronline.com/2020/02/16-ways-educators-can-help-young-children-self-reflect.html/

Kaiser, E. (2020, July 30). *What is self-awareness and why is it important.* Better Kids. https://betterkids.education/blog/what-is-self-awareness-and-why-is-it-important

Khan, A. (2024, March 19). *30 fun indoor and outdoor physical activities for kids.* First Cry. https://parenting.firstcry.com/articles/30-indoor-and-outdoor-physical-activities-for-kids/

Longenecker, D. (2019, June 17). *Enjoy adventure saying yes experience.* LinkedIn. https://www.linkedin.com/pulse/enjoy-adventure-saying-yes-new-experiences-douglas-longenecker/

Lorina. (2023, July 20). *Turning children's weaknesses into strengths.* Aussie Childcare Network. https://aussiechildcarenetwork.com.au/articles/child-behaviour/turning-children-s-weaknesses-into-strengths

MANLY. (2023, November). *Flying cars: The game-changing innovation.* MANLYBattery. https://manlybattery.com/flying-cars-the-game-changing-innovation/

Melissa. (2023, September 26). *7 tips for helping your child deal with bullying.* Hopkins Medicine. https://www.hopkinsmedicine.org/health/wellness-and-prevention/7-tips-for-helping-your-child-deal-with-bullying

Michalowicz, M. (2013, February 18). *5 easy steps to find your hidden talents.* Mike Michalowicz. https://mikemichalowicz.com/5-easy-steps-to-find-your-hidden-talents/

Mittal, M. (2024, May 10). *Teaching kids on how assess information accuracy?* LinkedIn. https://www.linkedin.com/pulse/teaching-kids-how-assess-information-accuracy-megha-mittal-2hqkf/

Modern Recovery Editorial Team. (n.d.). *Emotional awareness: Definition, benefits, and techniques.* Modern Recovery Services.

https://modernrecoveryservices.com/wellness/coping/skills/emotional/emotional-awareness/

MountsAdm. (2021, October 20). *10 effective tips for teaching children self-discipline.* Montessori Academy. https://montessori-academy.com/blog/10-effective-tips-for-teaching-children-self-discipline/

National Health Service. (2021, February 4). *Helping your child with anger issues.* https://www.nhs.uk/mental-health/children-and-young-adults/advice-for-parents/help-your-child-with-anger-issues/

National Health Service. (2023, January 4). *10 ways to fight your fears.* https://www.nhsinform.scot/healthy-living/mental-wellbeing/fears-and-phobias/10-ways-to-fight-your-fears/

Newman, T. (2017, August 8). *The secret to creating healthy eating habits in children.* Sanford Health News. https://news.sanfordhealth.org/healthy-living/the-secret-to-creating-healthy-eating-habits-in-children/

Perry, E. (2023, August 8). *The meaning of personal values: How they shape your life.* BetterUp. https://www.betterup.com/blog/meaning-of-personal-values

Pixeld. (2024, April). *How to teach kids to care for the environment and cultivate sustainable habits* Child's Play ELC. https://www.childsplayelc.com.au/how-to-teach-kids-to-care-for-the-environment-and-cultivate-sustainable-habits/

Problem facts for kids. (n.d.). Kiddle. https://kids.kiddle.co/Problem

Rai, A. (2023, July 8). *Introducing kids to the importance of self-introspection.* Ezyschooling.

https://ezyschooling.com/parenting/expert/introducing-kids-to-the-importance-of-self-introspection

Rosen, P. (n.d.). *Emotional intelligence in children.* Understood. https://www.understood.org/en/articles/the-importance-of-emotional-intelligence-for-kids-with-learning-and-thinking-differences

Selby. (2023, June 8). *Teaching adaptability and flexibility to elementary students.* Everyday Speech. https://everydayspeech.com/blog-posts/no-prep-social-skills-sel-activity/teaching-adaptability-and-flexibility-to-elementary-students/

7 things to teach your kids about internet safety. (n.d.). F-Secure. https://www.f-secure.com/en/articles/7-things-to-teach-your-kids-about-internet-safety

Singh, K. (2024, March 12). *Mastering art home chore management.* LinkedIn. https://www.linkedin.com/pulse/mastering-art-home-chore-management-guide-modern-kavi-singh-j9s6c/

Six steps to smarter studying. (n.d.). Kids Health. https://kidshealth.org/en/kids/studying.html

Turansky, S. (2020, January 14). *Parent to your child's strengths in order to address weaknesses.* Thriving Kids Connection. https://thrivingkidsconnection.com/parent-to-your-childs-strengths-in-order-to-address-weaknesses/

Vassel, J. (2020, October 13). *Tips to help kids embrace their uniqueness and practice self-love.* PBS SoCal. https://www.pbssocal.org/education/tips-help-kids-embrace-uniqueness-practice-self-love

What it means to be a good citizen and how to teach children. (2023, January 24). Lifespan. https://www.lifespan.org/lifespan-living/what-it-means-be-good-citizen-and-how-teach-children

What new technology, not yet existing, are you most looking forward to/hoping for? (n.d.). Quora. https://www.quora.com/What-new-technology-not-yet-existing-are-you-most-looking-forward-to-hoping-for

What to do when you feel sad. (n.d.). Kids Health. https://kidshealth.org/en/kids/depression.html

Webmaster. (2023, August). *Helping young citizens become good citizens.* Charity for Change. https://charityforchange.org/helping-young-citizens-become-good-citizens/

Your Feedback Matters

Thank you so much for choosing my book. I know there are countless options, so I appreciate you giving this one a chance.

As you've reached the end of the book, I hope it has provided you with valuable insights and ideas. Before you close this book, I would like to request a small favor. Your thoughts and feedback are critical to me.

Could you please consider sharing a review? Your review will support me as an independent author and help other readers discover this book.

Your feedback fuels my passion for writing and guides me in creating content that resonates with you. Your contribution is instrumental in my growth as an author. I am deeply appreciative of your time and the support you've shown by choosing my book.

Thank you once again for being a part of this journey!

LEAVE A REVIEW ON AMAZON:

United States

Canada

United Kingdom

Australia

India

Singapore

Printed in Great Britain
by Amazon

59293438R00175